AGATHA HETERODYNE & THE CIRCUS OF DREAMS

A Gaslamp Fantasy with ADVENTURE, ROMANCE & MAD SCIENCE

OTHER BOOKS FROM AIRSHIP ENTERTAINMENT AND STUDIO FOGLIO

YA 741.5 FOGLI

Girl Genius® Graphic Novels

Girl Genius Volume One:
Agatha Heterodyne and the Beetleburg Clank

Girl Genius Volume Two:
Agatha Heterodyne and the Airship City

Girl Genius Volume Three:
Agatha Heterodyne and the Monster Engine

Girl Genius Volume Four:
Agatha Heterodyne and the Circus of Dreams

Girl Genius Volume Five:
Agatha Heterodyne and the Clockwork Princess

Other Graphic Novels

What's New with Phil & Dixie Vol.s 1-3

Robert Asprin's MythAdventures®

Buck Godot, zap gun for hire:
- *Three Short Stories*
- *PSmIth*
- *The Gallimaufry*

Girl Genius® is published by:
Airship Entertainment™, a happy part of Studio Foglio, LLC
2400 NW 80th St #129 Seattle WA 98117-4449, USA

Please visit our Web sites at www.airshipbooks.com and www.girlgenius.net

Story by Phil & Kaja Foglio. Pencils by Phil Foglio. Main story colors by Laurie E. Smith. *Fan Fiction* written by Shaenon K. Garrity, with colors by Cheyenne Wright. Selected spot illos colored by Kaja Foglio and Cheyenne Wright. Logos, Lettering, Artist Bullying & Book Design by Kaja. Fonts mostly by Comicraft– www.comicbookfonts.com.

Much of the material in this collection was originally published in the Girl Genius comic book issues 10-13. The rest appeared three times a week at girlgenius.net April-June 2005.

Softcover Edition: ISBN#1-890856-36-3

Second Printing: August 2006 PRINTED IN HONG KONG

This book is dedicated to Marie Cooley and Payne Fifield, who are even more amazing than their cartoon avatars.

PHIL FOGLIO

Professor Foglio specializes in field research. His latest paper concludes that most of them are rectangular and need weeding. He is also an expert in the early life of Agatha Heterodyne, and is the author of the much-admired Jägermonster/Romanian dictionary and phrase book, "Hey Dere, Sveethøt." He has vowed to remain in the field until he can find his keys.

KAJA FOGLIO

Professor Foglio had the satisfaction of seeing her last paper chronicling the life of Agatha Heterodyne read aloud before the Academy of Letters and Egregious Punctuation for unprecedented mastery of the semi-colon. Disaster was narrowly averted earlier this year, when a newly refurbished Mr. Tock inexplicably attempted to hunt her down and step on her, doing quite a bit of damage to the campus of Transylvania Polygnostic before she was able to lure it out onto the then-frozen surface of Tozer-Kilts Pond. Baffled university engineers expressed amazement at "—how fast she could run in those shoes."

LAURIE E. SMITH

Continuing her experiments with blasphemous color theory, Professor Smith was the person responsible for turning the entire sky orange for several days last year—an incident noticed by surprisingly few people. She plans to continue her research until she finds a color she likes.

SHAENON K. GARRITY

Professor Garrity is known primarily for her own researches. These chronicle the life of girl mad scientist Helen Narbon, who inhabits a fascinating parallel world *quite different* from our own. Professor Garrity meticulously creates a new chapter of her chronicle every day, then electrifies it and claims that it spreads across the entire world via wires and glass. Sure. We will concede, however, that interesting results have been obtained by having our electro-mechanical Ouija boards spell out the mysterious phrase "www.narbonic.com"

CHEYENNE WRIGHT

Professor Wright was found emerging from a cave beneath Transylvania Polygnostic University several years ago, dressed in an outfit made from the skins of several hundred bats. The University Board, a cowardly and superstitious lot, immediately gave him tenure if he would only promise to stop "looking at them like that." He has been routinely mocked for his assertions that colors are composed entirely of numbers, but is greatly admired by the student body for his fashion sense. You can view the latest results of his work at www.arcanetimes.com.

OUR STORY THUS FAR

Agatha Clay is a Spark—capable of scientific wonders.

She has recently discovered that she is also the last of the famous Heterodyne family—

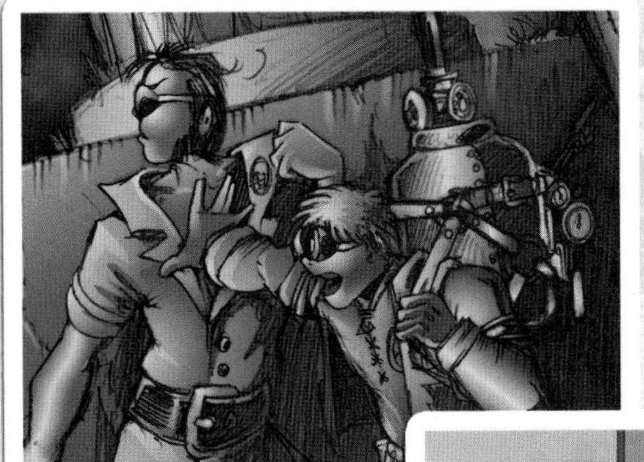

—heroes who disappeared mysteriously many years ago.

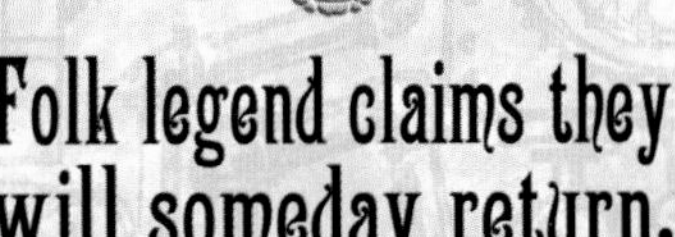

Folk legend claims they will someday return.

Agatha was raised by **Adam and Lilith Clay**—a pair of constructs built by her father and uncle.

Adam & Lilith are better known in stories of the Heterodynes as Punch and Judy.

The Clays have just helped Agatha escape from the giant airship Castle Wulfenbach; at the cost of their lives.

Also fleeing the Castle is Krosp—a failed experiment created to be the King of the Cats.

Castle Wulfenbach is the fortress of **Baron Klaus Wulfenbach**—an old companion of the Heterodynes who now rules Europe with an iron fist. The Baron would prefer to keep Agatha safely a prisoner.

The Baron's son Gilgamesh would also like her to stay, but he has other reasons.

And this is a Mimmoth.

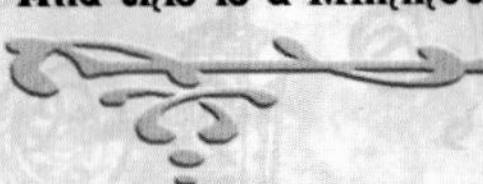

KROSP! WAKE UP!
MF. WHAT IS IT, AGATHA?
PURSUIT?
NO—WE'RE STARTING TO LOSE ALTITUDE.
PRETTY QUICKLY, TOO.
I DIDN'T THINK THAT PATCH WOULD HOLD.
CAN WE CLEAR THAT PEAK?
I'M GOING TO TRY.

AIM FOR THE FIELD!
I'LL AIM FOR THE POND!
NO!
ANYTHING BUT THAT!
HEY! WHAT ARE YOU DOING?!
LET GO!
PWANG!
TONG
KRUNCH
AAAAAAAAAAAAAAAAAAAAAAAA
AGATHA, ARE YOU OKAY?
UHHHHH... YES.
CAN YOU MOVE?
TINK
PING!
POP
I...I THINK SO.
THEN GET OFF ME!!
LOOK AT THIS!
IT'S COMPLETELY DESTROYED!
WHY DIDN'T YOU LET ME LAND IN THE POND?
JEEZ, THEN I'D HAVE GOTTEN WET.

WELL, SO MUCH FOR TRAVELING EASILY.
COME ON, LET'S SEE WHAT WE'VE GOT.
HEY-*HEY!*
WHAT?
THAT THING WE COULDN'T OPEN? *WEAPONS LOCKER!*
THEY LOOK PRETTY MESSED UP.
CAN YOU FIX 'EM?
I DON'T KNOW.
THERE WERE SOME TOOLS ON THE SHIP...
I'LL SEE WHAT I CAN DO.
RIGHT THEN. *YOU* GET TO WORK.
I'LL GET EVERYTHING WE CAN USE AND TRY TO COVER THE WRECKAGE A BIT.
SOON...
LET'S GO.
I WANT US FAR AWAY BEFORE THE BARON'S PEOPLE SHOW UP.
OKAY. I THINK I'VE GOT SOMETHING.
YEAH? LET'S SEE.
F-TAM!
BEAUTIFUL.
VERY... IMPRESSIVE.
NICE HETERODYNE SIGIL.
IT WAS IN LILITH'S PACK.
I FIGURED IF WE'RE GOING TO BE WANDERING STRANGERS, WE SHOULD AT *LEAST* LOOK LIKE WE'RE *GOOD GUYS*.
AFTER ALL, WE MAY NEED HELP SOON. THERE WASN'T MUCH ON THE AIRSHIP.
WE'VE GOT THE GUN, MEDICAL SUPPLIES AND A LITTLE FOOD.
NOT NEARLY ENOUGH. IT WON'T LAST LONG.
WE'LL EAT WHAT I CATCH, AND SAVE WHAT'S IN THE PACK FOR AN EMERGENCY.
I THOUGHT YOU'VE NEVER BEEN OFF *CASTLE WULFENBACH*.
HEY, CATS ARE *NATURAL* HUNTERS.
C'MON. WE'LL HIDE IN THAT GRASS.
...THOSE ARE *TREES.*
WHATEVER.

LATER—

COME ON, HAVE A SAUSAGE.

OBVIOUSLY, I'M *NOT HUNGRY.*

OF *COURSE* I WILL.

WHEN I'M *REALLY* HUNGRY.

HEY. HUNTING OUT IN THE REAL WORLD IS *DIFFERENT.*

YOU'LL GET SOMETHING *EVENTUALLY.*

WELL, MAYBE WE CAN FIND A FARM WE CAN—

NO! THEY'D ASK TOO MANY QUESTIONS.

AND THEY'D *REMEMBER* US.

PEOPLE LOOK AFTER THEIR OWN FIRST.

WHEN THE BARON COMES LOOKING, WE'RE SAUS—

ER...

STRANGERS.

THEY OWE US *NOTHING.*

WE'LL LET THINGS DIE DOWN A BIT.

WHEN WE RUN OUT OF SAUS—

UH... *SUPPLIES,*

THEN WE TRY TO GET HELP.

WELL, THAT'S AS GOOD A PLAN AS *ANY,* I SUPPOSE.

GOODNIGHT, O MIGHTY HUNTER.

MMMF.

ZZ
OOF!
RRROWRAGH!
BREAKFAST!!
YEAH! CAUGHT BY ME!!
MROWR!
NOW EAT UP!
HA!
ERG. I...I THOUGHT YOU WANTED TO GET MOVING.
WELL, YEAH.
WELL, I'LL JUST EAT WHAT I'VE GOT IN THE PACK.
WHAT?! BUT I CAUGHT YOU FOOD!
ME! SEE? HERE!
I'M NOT EATING THIS!... ER...RAW.
MM. I DON'T WANT TO WASTE TIME COOKING... BUT...
LOOK, TODAY I'LL EAT FROM THE PACK.
TONIGHT YOU CAN CATCH EXTRA—
—AND I'LL ROAST IT OVERNIGHT IN THE COALS.
WELL...
—AND I KNOW YOU CAN DO IT,
CAUSE YOU'RE OBVIOUSLY AN AMAZING HUNTING CREATURE.
...YEAH?
OH, YES.
WELL... OKAY.
BUT YOU DON'T KNOW WHAT YOU'RE MISSING.
THE HEAD IS BEST RAW.
CRONCH
CRONCH
SOMEHOW, I'LL LIVE.
SOB

DID YOU HEAR THAT?
YES.
WHY, IT'S JUST A LITTLE KID.
AAAH!
SCARED, TOO.
RELAX, WE'RE NOT GOING TO HURT YOU.
WHERE ARE YOUR PARENTS?
I... I DON'T KNOW!
I WAS PLAYING,
AND NOW I CAN'T FIND MY WAY BACK.
REALLY.
WELL, WELL.
OUR SEARCH FOR PROVISIONS MIGHT BE OVER.
KROSP!
SMEK!
WE'RE "GOOD GUYS," REMEMBER?
YOU'LL SCARE HIM!
WHAT?!
HE'S IN A TREE! MAYBE HE'S A BIRD!
HE'S NOT A BIRD.
SQUIRREL!
HEE HEE!
I DIDN'T KNOW YOU WERE SHOW PEOPLE!
SHOW PEOPLE?
YEAH! THAT'S A GREAT TALKING CAT ACT!
HIT HIM AGAIN!
I MIGHT.
HEY!
ARE YOUR PARENTS SHOW PEOPLE?
YUP. MASTER PAYNE'S CIRCUS OF ADVENTURE.
TELL YOUR FRIENDS.
SO YOU DON'T LIVE AROUND HERE.
NOPE!
JUST PASSING THROUGH LIKE CHEAP BEER!
I BEG YOUR PARDON?
THAT'S WHAT MY DADDY SAYS.
HE PLAYS PUNCH A LOT.
YOU CAN MEET HIM WHEN YOU TAKE ME HOME!
UM, WE'LL TRY.
I SMELL CAMPFIRES, AND HORSES AND PEOPLE.
OVER THAT WAY, KID.

LET'S GET YOU BACK TO YOUR FOLKS.
HUZZAH!
HEY! NO PEOPLE! REMEMBER?
I'M NOT GOING TO SEND HIM OFF BY HIMSELF.
WHY NOT? HE GOT HERE BY HIMSELF!
THAT IS THE GREATEST CAT EVER!
THIS MUST BE IT.
YEAH! THAT'S OUR WAGON!
BALTHAZAR!

BALTHAZAR!
MAMA! I GOT LOST!
HE'S YOURS, THEN. GOOD.
YES! THANK YOU!
I WAS SO WORRIED!
WE FOUND HIM SITTING IN A TREE.
I'M AGATHA CLAY.
TRISH BELLOPTRIX.
SHE'S NICE, MAMA! SHE'S SHOW PEOPLE!

SHOW PEOPLE?
YEAH! SHE'S GOT A GREAT TALKING CAT ACT!
CAT ACT.
HEY, HOWZIT GOING?
THAT'S YOUR "ACT" IS IT?
ER...HE CALLED IT AN ACT.
NOT ME.
AND I DANCE, TOO.
VOH DOH-DEE-OH-DOH...
HA. DON'T WORRY.
HE'S CUTE. THE TOWNIES MUST LOVE HIM.
WHY DON'T YOU COME WITH ME?
WE WERE STARTING BREAKFAST WHEN I MISSED BALTHAZAR.
A MEAL IS THE LEAST I CAN DO.
WELL, I DON'T WANT TO BE A BOTHER...BUT...
FOOD. YEAH. FOOD IS ALWAYS GOOD.
...DARN RIGHT, I'M CUTE.
WHERE'S THE REST OF YOUR PARTY?
UM...IT'S JUST US.
YOU'RE WALKING AROUND THE WASTELANDS ALONE?!
WE WERE IN AN AIRSHIP, BUT IT CRASHED.
SO—YOU'RE SOME KIND OF ADVENTURER.
WHY, THEN, IT MUST BE LUCK THAT BROUGHT YOU HERE!
LUCK?
YES! FOR HERE YOU WILL FIND THE GREATEST DISSEMBLANCE OF HEROES IN ALL OF EUROPE!
WHAT?

THAT'S "ASSEMBLAGE" DEAR.
RIGHT.
WHAT?
HOY! YOU FOUND HIM!
IT'S A TRAVELING HETERODYNE SHOW.
THIS IS MISS AGATHA CLAY.
MISS CLAY?, THIS IS ABNER.
MASTER PAYNE'S ASSISTANT.
WHERE DID SHE COME FROM?
HETERODYNE?
SURE, IT'S...OH. OH MY.
SHE BROUGHT BALTHAZAR BACK.
AH.
MASTER PAYNE WANTS US READY TO MOVE ON AS SOON AS POSSIBLE.
THERE'S... SOMETHING OUT THERE THAT'S SPOOKING THE HORSES.
WAS THAT CAT TALKING?
OH. YES.
...INTERESTING.
I'D BETTER GO TELL EVERYONE BALTHAZAR'S BEEN FOUND.
I PROMISED HER A MEAL, BUT MASTER PAYNE MIGHT LET HER JOIN UP—
—IF ONLY BECAUSE SHE'S TRAVELING SOLO.
SOLO?! IN THE WASTELANDS?!
IT WASN'T MY IDEA. MY AIRSHIP CRASHED.
AIRSHIP CRASH, WEIRD GUN, TALKING CAT.
YOU'LL FIT RIGHT IN AROUND HERE.
YOU WOULDN'T KNOW ANYTHING ABOUT WHATEVER IS OUT THERE, WOULD YOU?
SORRY, NO.
WHOA! YOU SMELL THAT?
SO—YOU WERE THE ONLY SURVIVORS?
OH, NO. NOTHING LIKE THAT—
—IT WAS JUST US ON BOARD.
AN AIRSHIP CREWED BY ONE...AND A HALF?
THAT'S A SMALL CRAFT FOR OUT HERE.
WHERE WERE YOU COMING FROM?
COULD BE.
IS IT IMPORTANT?
I SAW A WULFENBACH SIGIL ON YOUR PACK, THERE.
I KNOW CASTLE WULFENBACH'S IN THESE PARTS—
FOLKS WERE TALKING ABOUT IT IN THE LAST TOWN.
SO I'M GUESSING YOU'RE OFF THE CASTLE.
YOU WORK FOR THE BARON?

NO! I MEAN, WELL, I GUESS I DID. FOR A WHILE.
BUT NOT ANYMORE. UH HUH.
SO YOU'RE ON THE RUN, THEN.
HOO BOY.
WULFENBACH, EH? HE'S TROUBLE, THAT ONE.
I DIDN'T HURT ANYONE. I JUST...LEFT.
LOOKS LIKE YOU "JUST LEFT" IN A HURRY.
HOW DID YOU ESCAPE?
MY PARENTS. THEY...THEY CAME TO GET ME BUT THEY...IT WAS HORRIBLE.
I ESCAPED IN THE CONFUSION.
I STILL CAN'T BELIEVE THEY'RE DEAD.
THEY'LL BE LOOKING FOR YOU.
WHEN WAS THIS?
YESTERDAY. IT WAS ONLY YESTERDAY. I CAN'T BELIEVE...
YOU POOR KID. I'M SURE WE COULD—
DON'T YOU SAY ANOTHER WORD.
WHAT?
THIS IS IMPORTANT. AND IT'S MASTER PAYNE'S DECISION. NOT YOURS.
I WAS JUST—
JUST ABOUT TO SAY SOMETHING STUPID!
GET MASTER PAYNE!
I DIDN'T MEAN TO CAUSE ANY TROUBLE...

HA. *YOU* DIDN'T.
THOSE TWO HAVE BEEN LIKE THAT WITH EACH OTHER SINCE PIX JOINED UP.
SHE'S A *GREAT* ACTRESS, THOUGH.
HERE, EAT UP. I'M ZEETHA.
OH. I'M AGATHA.
YOU REALLY ESCAPED FROM CASTLE WULFENBACH?
YES.
GOOD FOR YOU. YOU'RE TOUGHER THAN YOU LOOK.
I HAD HELP.
SO?
MY PEOPLE SAY THAT A GOOD FRIEND IS A STRONG SWORD.
YOUR PEOPLE?
I'M FROM SKIFANDER. EVER HEAR OF IT?
SKIFANDER?
OH, YES. THE "WARRIOR QUEEN'S HIDDEN JEWEL".
I'M SORRY... DID I GET IT WRONG? IT'S BEEN SO LONG.
WHO TAUGHT YOU THAT!?
DO YOU KNOW WHERE SKIFANDER *IS!?*
WHAT? *NO!*
MY...MY UNCLE! HE USED TO TELL ME *STORIES!*
WHERE IS HE?
I DON'T KNOW!
HE DISAPPEARED *YEARS* AGO!

NO!
NO!
FINALLY, SOMEONE, AND—NO!
NO NO NO!
SHHYNG
NOOOOO!
CHOP CHOP
CHOP CHOP CHOP
CHOP
CHOP
CHOP
CHOP CHOP
AAAAAHHH!!
SHE'S NEVER DONE THAT A'FORE...
WHAT THE DEVIL WAS THAT ALL ABOUT?
THEY WERE JUST TALKING, AND THEN ZEETHA WENT NUTS!
WHAT HAPPENED?
I DON'T KNOW! WE WERE TALKING ABOUT SKIFANDER AND-
YOU'VE HEARD OF SKIFANDER? REALLY?
WELL, YES! BUT...WHY?

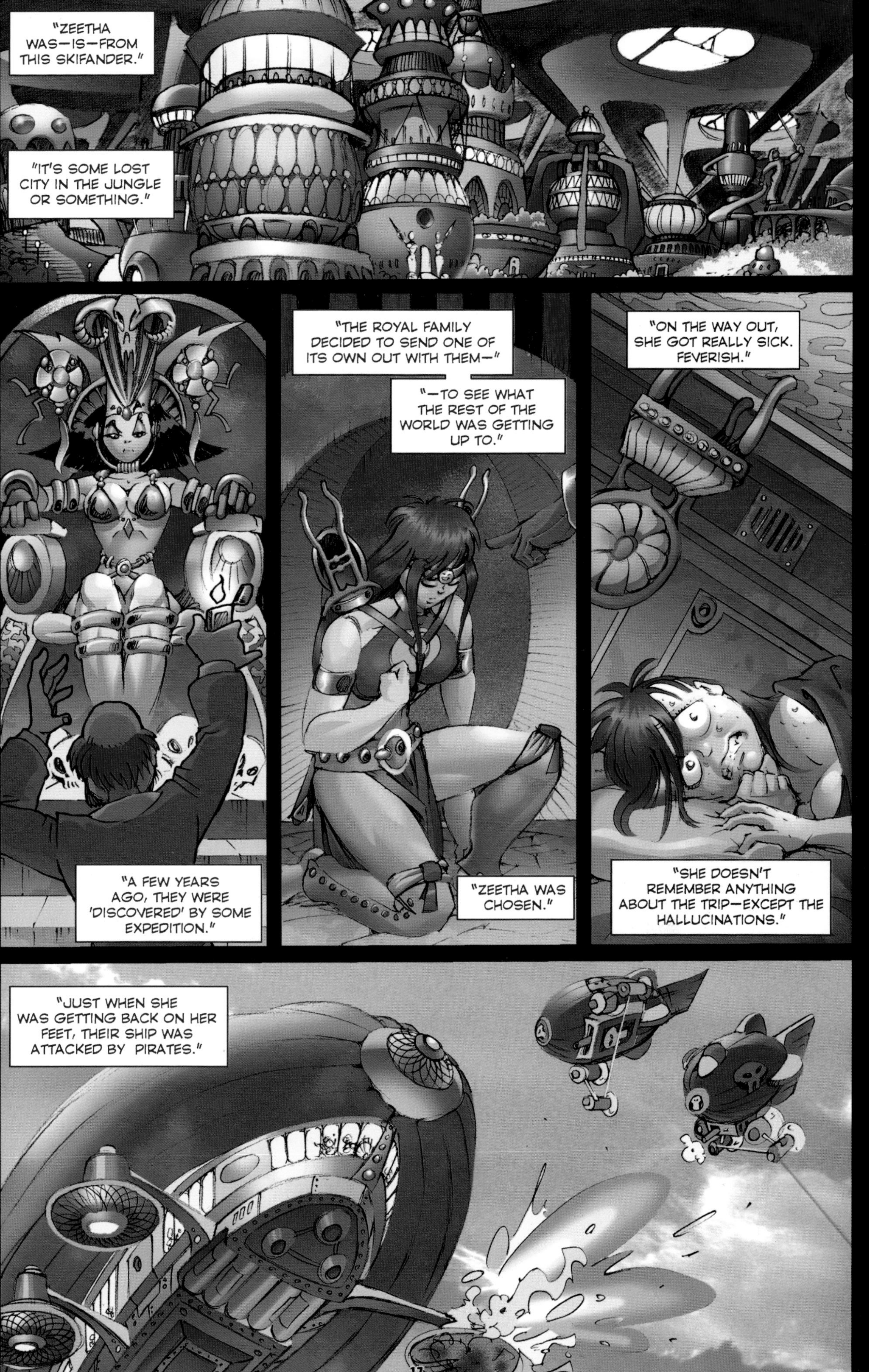
"ZEETHA WAS—IS—FROM THIS SKIFANDER."
"IT'S SOME LOST CITY IN THE JUNGLE OR SOMETHING."
"A FEW YEARS AGO, THEY WERE 'DISCOVERED' BY SOME EXPEDITION."
"THE ROYAL FAMILY DECIDED TO SEND ONE OF ITS OWN OUT WITH THEM—"
"—TO SEE WHAT THE REST OF THE WORLD WAS GETTING UP TO."
"ZEETHA WAS CHOSEN."
"ON THE WAY OUT, SHE GOT REALLY SICK. FEVERISH."
"SHE DOESN'T REMEMBER ANYTHING ABOUT THE TRIP—EXCEPT THE HALLUCINATIONS."
"JUST WHEN SHE WAS GETTING BACK ON HER FEET, THEIR SHIP WAS ATTACKED BY PIRATES."

"THEY KILLED EVERYONE ELSE ON BOARD, BUT TOOK ZEETHA PRISONER."
"FOUND HER HAIR EXOTIC, I GUESS."
"THEY PLANNED ON SELLING HER, SO THEY TOOK REASONABLY GOOD CARE OF HER—"
"—THOUGH SHE WAS STILL LOCKED UP."
"BY THE TIME THEY GOT HER BACK TO THEIR FORTRESS, SHE WAS NICE AND HEALTHY."
"WELL, SHE WIPED OUT ALL OF THE PIRATES ON THE SHIP—"
"—AND THEN ALL THE SHIPS IN THE FLEET,"
"AND HAD JUST FINISHED OFF THEIR FORTRESS WHEN SHE REALIZED SHE'D KILLED EVERYONE WHO MIGHT HAVE KNOWN ***WHERE*** SHE'D BEEN PICKED UP."
SMEK
ARGH!

SINCE THEN, SHE'S BEEN WANDERING AND SEARCHING FOR A WAY HOME.
SHE JOINED UP WITH US ABOUT TWO YEARS AGO.
YOU'RE THE FIRST PERSON WHO'S EVEN **HEARD** OF THIS "SKIFANDER."
THE POOR THING. I WISH I KNEW MORE.
AGATHA, MASTER PAYNE WANTS TO SEE YOU.
GOTTA PACK. NICE MEETING YOU.
SO—WHERE ARE YOU HEADING?
MECHANICSBURG.
HUH. QUITE A WAY. YOU HAVE FAMILY THERE?
THAT'S WHAT I'M GOING TO FIND OUT.
YOUR BEST BET IS TO HEAD WEST.
EVENTUALLY, YOU'LL HIT THE **DANUBE**.
FOLLOW IT EAST.
SCREEE-POK! SCREEE-POK!
RIGHT. UM...
WHAT THE HELL IS IT **NOW?!**
EXCUSE ME, BUT THAT NOISE MEANS YOUR GYRO GEAR NEEDS RE-PACKING.
WHAT?
AHA! SEE, I **TOLD** YOU!
AH, WHAT DOES **SHE** KNOW?
I KNOW **THAT'S** A DUTCHY OF BLENSHAF **GYRO WHEEL**.
YOUR WOBBLE PLATE IS **LOOSE**—
—IT SOUNDS LIKE YOU'VE NEGLECTED TO REPLACE THE SPONGE DAMPERS—
—**AND** YOU DON'T HAVE THE CORRECT FORMULA FOR **TREAD GUNK**.

YOU KNOW GYRO WHEELS.
MY DAD WAS A SMITH.
WE SAW THESE ALL THE TIME.
YOU WANT A JOB?
WHAT?
ME AND RIVET, WE'RE PISTON LEG MEN.
THIS BLASTED WHEEL'S GOT US SMOKED.
PROFESS AND UNIQUE FLEA
WE COULD USE ANOTHER MECHANIC AROUND HERE ANYWAY.
I DON'T THINK THAT'S A GOOD IDEA.
YES. I'VE GOT TO GET TO MECHANICSBURG.
SO WHAT'S THE PROBLEM?
WE'LL BE PASSING RIGHT THROUGH MECHANICSBURG.
sigh.
...REALLY.
SURE! IT'LL TAKE A FEW MONTHS, BUT YOU'LL EARN—
RIVET, SHUT UP!
WHAT? BUT PIX, WHAT'S THE PROBLEM?
THE PROBLEM IS THAT MISS CLAY CANNOT TRAVEL WITH US.

MISS CLAY. I AM *MASTER PAYNE.*
I AM SORRY TO BE SO BLUNT. YOU DID US A FAVOR, AND WE *ARE* GRATEFUL.
BUT THIS IS *MY* CIRCUS, AND *I* AM RESPONSIBLE FOR THE SAFETY OF THE PEOPLE IN IT.
OUR ROADS DIVERGE HERE.

WHAT'S WRONG WITH HER?
SHE'S ON THE RUN FROM *CASTLE WULFENBACH.*
EVEN ORDINARY TOWNSFOLK MIGHT BE PUNISHED SIMPLY FOR *AIDING* HER—
—AND WE HAVE OUR *OWN* CONCERNS, AS YOU WELL KNOW.
WE DON'T WANT ANY TROUBLE FROM THE BARON.
MISS CLAY, THE BEST WE CAN DO IS TO FORGET WE EVER SAW YOU.
AND WISH YOU LUCK.

I DO UNDERSTAND.
I'D BETTER LEAVE RIGHT AWAY, THEN.
GOODBYE, PIX. I WISH—
GOODBYE, ABNER.
C'MON, KROSP.
HMF. LEAST YOU COULD'VE DONE WAS GIVE HER A KIND WORD.
WHY? SHE'S DOOMED.
DIDN'T YOU HEAR?
SHE'S IN THE WASTELANDS. ALONE!
I LIKED HER TOO. SHE SEEMED NICE.
BUT I DON'T WANT TO GET NEAR WULFENBACH OR ANYBODY LIKE HIM.
NO MATTER HOW NICE SHE IS,
SHE'D BRING HIM AND HIS MONSTERS RIGHT DOWN ON OUR HEADS.
SHE CAN'T STAY AND SHE'LL DIE IF SHE GOES.
I HAVEN'T ANY KINDNESS LEFT FOR THE DEAD!
BUT COULDN'T WE—
OH, YOU'RE SUCH AN IDIOT!
THE COUNTESS WILL GIVE ME HELL OVER THIS, BUT PIX IS RIGHT.
NOW, LET'S GET OUT OF HERE.

WELL, *THAT* COULD HAVE GONE BETTER.
AGATHA?
YOU OKAY?
NO.
I KNOW YOU SAID THAT PEOPLE WOULD LOOK AFTER THEIR OWN,
BUT I NEVER THOUGHT WE COULD *HARM* PEOPLE JUST BY *TALKING* TO THEM.
WELL, WE WERE PLANNING ON AVOIDING PEOPLE *ANYWAY.*
I KNOW. BUT THE WAY THEY WERE TALKING ABOUT THE WASTELANDS—
—KROSP, I DON'T KNOW IF WE CAN *DO* THIS ALONE.
I DON'T SEE THAT WE HAVE A LOT OF *CHOICE.*
NO.
NO CHOICE AT ALL, REALLY.

RHREEE!
WHAT THE—
IT'S THE CIRCUS!
RHREEE RHREEE!
THEY'RE IN TROUBLE!
WOW. THAT'S NOT GOOD.
FWAAAP!
DON'T THEY HAVE ANY DEFENSES?
THEY'RE SCATTERING LIKE GEESE!
THAT'S WHAT WAS OUT IN THE WOODS!
WHAT'LL WE DO!?

THEY'RE COMING *THIS WAY!*
RUN!!
NO! I'VE GOT TO *HELP!*
ARE YOU *CRAZY?!*
YOU'LL BE *KILLED!*

CLAK!
F-TAM!
KRACK!
AAAAAHH!!

RHREEE!
HEY! OVER HERE!
NOOOOO!!
F-TAM!
BWAM!

IT'S STILL GOING!
I HIT THE MAIN ENGINE.
IT'S *FINISHED!*
IT JUST DOESN'T *KNOW* IT YET!
SNAP!
CRACKLE!
ZOK!
POP! POP!
YOU! GET UP!
GET UP!
GET—
AH!
OH, OLGA. OH *NO!*
CHAK-AK!
YAA!
EEP!

CHAK
LOOK OUT!
PAF!
WHAT—?
FWAAA!

BOOM!
RRRR KE-SMASH!

AGATHA!!
SSSSSSSSs

MEMORIES—
YOU WHAT?!
NO NEED TO SHOUT, DARLING.
I'M GOING TO MARRY BILL HETERODYNE.
HE ASKED ME YESTERDAY.
LUCREZIA, ARE YOU OUT OF YOUR MIND?
OH, YOU'RE SO SWEET.
I KNEW YOU'D TAKE IT HARD.
BUT I'M GOING TO DO IT.
I'M GOING TO RENOUNCE MY FATHER'S WORK AND JOIN UP WITH THE "GOOD GUYS."

OH, AND I DON'T COUNT, THEN?
OH, KLAUS. YOU MAY WORK WITH THEM—
—BUT YOU HAVE FAR TOO MUCH OF A DARK SIDE OF YOUR OWN.
SO DO YOU.
I KNOW. IT'S WHAT YOU LIKE ABOUT ME, ISN'T IT?
ONE OF THE THINGS...
NOW, BILL KNOWS I'M BAD.
BUT HE THINKS I CAN CHANGE.
HE'S WRONG. THEY THINK THAT ABOUT EVERYBODY.
I KNOW YOU TOO WELL.
YOU'LL BE BORED OUT OF YOUR MIND, AND YOU'LL TRY SOMETHING.
IN FACT, THIS IS PROBABLY ALL ONE OF YOUR SCHEMES RIGHT NOW, ISN'T IT?
WHAT ARE YOU REALLY UP TO?
NO, KLAUS, THIS ISN'T A GAME.
I AM DETERMINED TO CHANGE.
I DO LOVE HIM. IT SHOULD BE ENOUGH.
BESIDES, THEY ALWAYS WIN.
THERE MUST BE SOMETHING TO THEIR PHILOSOPHY.
THIS ISN'T ABOUT PHILOSOPHY.
BILL IS MY FRIEND. I WON'T LET YOU—

IS THAT HOW YOU PLAN TO CHANGE MY MIND?
BY SHOUTING AT ME?
OH, KLAUS. I WILL MISS YOU.
BUT I'M AFRAID I SIMPLY CAN'T HAVE YOU AROUND COMPLICATING THINGS.
IF ONLY BY BEING SUCH A TEMPTATION...
I'M AFRAID YOU REALLY WILL HAVE TO GO.
HAH! ANGHOWR 'DJER THIRG YG—
BY DRNG. HYU PZIND BY DRING.
NOT POISON, SILLY.
I'M ONE OF THE GOOD GUYS NOW, REMEMBER?
GOODBYE, DARLING.

YOU WANTED TO SEE ME, FATHER?
IDIOT!
HOW LONG DID YOU KNOW THAT THE GIRL WAS THE SPARK?
I SUSPECTED IT BACK IN BEETLEBURG.
I KNEW THIS MORNING.
WELL, NOW I KNOW IT TOO—AND SHE IS GONE!
WITH OTHAR NO LESS.
HE CAN WAIT, BUT—
—YOU WILL TAKE DuPREE AND THE TWO OF YOU WILL FIND THIS GIRL AND BRING HER BACK.

FATHER, I CAN'T JUST GRAB HER AND DRAG HER BACK HERE.
SHE'S A SPARK, BUT SHE HASN'T BROKEN THE PEACE.
YOU MOST CERTAINLY CAN!
SHE IS A HETERODYNE!
HER VERY EXISTENCE THREATENS THE PEACE!
PLUS, SHE IS THE DAUGHTER OF LUCREZIA MONGFISH.
THAT ALONE WARRANTS OUR ATTENTION.
FATHER, SHE'S ALREADY ANGRY WITH ME. IF I—
YOU WILL BRING HER BACK HERE.
AS A PRISONER.
IS THIS UNDERSTOOD?
IF I CAN JUST TALK TO HER, SHE MIGHT—
AS A PRISONER.
YOU CAN SAVE ANY ROMANTIC IDEAS YOU HAVE FOR LATER.
FOR NOW, JUST BRING HER BACK.
NOW GO. DuPREE IS WAITING ON DOCK 43.
YES, FATHER.

HEY! OVER HERE!
clik
I DID WHAT YOU WANTED—
—PRETENDED I WAS THE SPARK—
—YOU SAID YOU'D HELP ME.
YES. YES, I DID.
HERE. TAKE THIS.
GREAT! WHAT IS IT?
POISON. IT'LL KILL YOU INSTANTLY.
WHAT?!
GET AWAY FROM ME!
YOU'RE CRAZY!
I'M TRULY SORRY, MR. VON ZINZER.
I REALLY AM TRYING TO HELP YOU.
CASTLE HETERODYNE
I KNOW IT ISN'T MUCH—
—BUT THE WAY THINGS HAVE GONE—
—THIS SEEMS TO BE THE BEST I CAN DO.
I'M AFRAID IT MAY BE MORE THAN I CAN DO FOR MISS CLAY.

WELCOME, LADIES AND GENTLEMEN— TO A SHOW LIKE NO OTHER!
IT IS TRUE THAT WE BRING YOU THE USUAL AMUSEMENTS—
—SLEIGHT OF HAND, THRILLS, JOKES BOTH CHEAP AND WITTY—
—BUT THESE CAN BE HAD FROM ANY RAGTAG TROUPE OR TWOPENNY DREADFUL—
—AND I CAN SEE THAT YOU ARE AN AUDIENCE THAT DEMANDS MORE!
AND WE SHALL PROVIDE IT!
FOR TONIGHT, WE BRING YOU A STORY OF THE HETERODYNES!
—A STORY OF BRAVE HEROES!
—DASTARDLY VILLAINS!
—AND MONSTERS BOTH HUMAN AND NON!
ALL SET AGAINST A BACKGROUND OF BLOOD AND THUNDER!
TRAGEDY, SUBTERFUGE, REVELATIONS AND TRUE LOVE!
—LAUGHTER AND TEARS!
—SCIENCE AND MAGIC!
FOR BEFORE YOU TONIGHT IS THAT GLITTERING COMPANY—
—KNOWN THROUGHOUT THE WORLD AND BEYOND AS—
MASTER PAYNE'S CIRCUS OF ADVENTURE
BUT BEFORE TONIGHT'S MAIN SHOW—
OUR OWN PROFESSORS MOONSOCK AND THERM—
—WILL SHARE A SONG THEY LEARNED ON THEIR LAST TRIP TO THE AMERICAS!

SO-HOW DO THINGS LOOK?
...YES! WE HAVE NO BANANAS...
A GOOD CROWD, SIR. THE WHOLE TOWN IS HERE.
WE'RE ALMOST OUT OF "MIMMOTHS ON A STICK."
AND THE TROUPE?
ON EDGE—
THEY'LL BE ALL RIGHT ONCE THE SHOW GETS GOING.
HOW ARE YOU DOING?
IT'S—IT'S LIKE A STORM'S BREWING.
Scene 8
Scene 7
Scene 6
I KNOW SOMETHING IS GOING TO HAPPEN.
I JUST WANT TO GET IT OVER WITH.
BE CAREFUL WHAT YOU WISH FOR.
NO MATTER WHAT COMES—
—I THINK WE HAVE A CHANCE—
—AS LONG AS IT'S SOMETHING WE CAN GET TO LISTEN TO US.
BUT HEY, YOU NEVER KNOW!
MAYBE NOTHING WILL HAPPEN.
DO YOU REALLY BELIEVE THAT?
NO SIR.
GOOD LAD.
BECAUSE IT'S SHOWTIME.

ATTENTION!
EVERYONE IS TO STAY WHERE THEY ARE.
COOPERATE AND NO ONE WILL BE HARMED.
WULFENBACH.
WULFENBACH.
WULFENBACH.
WULFENBACH.
WULFENBACH.
WULFENBACH.
WULFENBACH.
WULFENBACH.
WULFENBACH.

NOT BE *HARMED?!*
HOW AM I SUPPOSED TO *WORK* HERE?
THESE PEOPLE MAY KNOW *NOTHING.*
OH, DON'T START *THAT* AGAIN.
I FOUND THE CRASH SITE—
—THE PLACE SHE SLEPT—
—AND TRACKS OF A CARAVAN GOING *RIGHT PAST* ON THE *SAME DAY.*
FOLLOW THE TRACKS, AND IEY-PRESTO, A TRAVELING SHOW!
SHE'S *HERE.*
I *KNOW* YOU'RE GOOD,
BUT *THIS TIME* WE WANT THE JOB DONE *WITHOUT INCIDENT.*
IT'S NOT *MY* FAULT IF I'M ALWAYS SENT AGAINST *UNREASONABLE PEOPLE.*
JUST *FIND* HER.
THEN *LET* ME *WORK!*

SO! YOU LOOK LIKE YOU THINK YOU'RE SMART!
WHO'S IN CHARGE HERE?
ER—YOU ARE.
WOW! YOU'RE SO SMART—
—I'LL JUST SLAP THIS GUY AROUND INSTEAD!
DuPREE—
HEY! I'M WORKING HERE!
DO I COME TO YOUR LAB AND TELL YOU HOW TO TORTURE RATS?
FREQUENTLY.
SO I KNOW WHAT I'M DOING! NOW—
WHAT DO YOU WANT?
OH. RIGHT.
WE'RE LOOKING FOR A GIRL. YOUNG. BLONDE. WEARS GLASSES.
CAUSED A LOT OF TROUBLE ON CASTLE WULFENBACH A COUPLE DAYS AGO.
GET EVERYONE OUT HERE WHERE WE CAN SEE THEM.

BUT SHE ISN'T HERE. ND I'M ONLY IN CHARGE OF THE SHOW.
THE VILLAGERS—
TOO MANY DETAILS.
LESSON TIME!
BZZAT!
OH YEAH! THIS THING IS GREAT!
WOOHOO!
THAT IS A MEDICAL EVICE, NOT A WEAPON!
SO I TWEAKED IT A BIT. I LIKE IT BETTER THIS WAY.
AB!
I DIDN'T BUILD IT SO YOU COULD—
LOOK—IS THIS THE GIRL?
OF COURSE NOT!
IS HE DEAD?
I SAID NO ONE WOULD BE HARMED!
"IF THEY OBEY."
GIVE THEM A CHANCE!

ISN'T THAT ALWAYS THE WAY?
MANAGEMENT THINKING IT KNOWS WHAT WORKS IN THE FIELD?
WHY, IF I WERE HERE ALONE—
—AND YOU PEOPLE WERE STILL STANDING AROUND—
—HALF OF YOU'D BE DEAD!
EVERYBODY LINE UP!
OY!
HEY!
THERE SHE GOES!
A-HA! SHE TRIED TO HIDE WITH THE VILLAGERS!
SHE'S MADE A BREAK FOR IT!
AAAAND—YEAH! CLANK GOT HER!
AMAZING. I DIDN'T BELIEVE—
OH-HO. NOW, YOU'RE NOT GOING TO TRY ANYTHING STUPID, ARE YOU?
ERK!
YOUR PROBLEM IS YOU'RE STILL THINKING "FIANCÉE."
THE WORD YOU WANT IS "PRISONER."
SHE WON'T LIKE IT, BUT HEY—
SHE OBVIOUSLY DIDN'T LIKE "FIANCÉE" MUCH, EITHER.
SO WHAT DO YOU SAY ABOUT MY METHODS NOW, HM?
SHUT UP.
CLANK—PUT HER DOWN. GENTLY.

IT'S NOT HER.
WHAT?!
GIRL, YES. LONDE, YES. MISS CLAY, NO.
YOU DON'T KNOW THAT!
SHE COULD BE IN DISGUISE!
YOU— WHAT'S YOUR NAME?
IT'S NOT HER.
BUT SHE RAN!
YES, THAT S PUZZLING.
YOU'D THINK WE WERE CRAZY PEOPLE WITH GUNS.
AND BATTLE CLANKS.
AND A GREAT BIG LOOMING
WHAT COULD POSSIBLY— AH...
THOSE SHOES.
THEY BELONG TO THE PERSON WE'RE LOOKING FOR.
WHERE IS SHE?

OH, THE MADGIRL!
JEEZ—I WAS SCARED YOU WERE LOOKIN' FOR JUST ANY OLD BLONDE!
WHEW!
YEAH! WE MET HER ON THE ROAD!
SHE WANTED TO TRAVEL WITH US—
—BUT WE KNEW SHE WAS SOME SORT OF CRIMINAL—
'CAUSE SHE SAID SHE WAS RUNNING FROM THE BARON!
WE DIDN'T DARE TRY TO CATCH HER FOR YOU, 'CAUSE SHE HAD THIS BIG GUN!
NOW, WE KNEW THERE WAS SOMETHING OUT IN THE WOODS—
—SOMETHING BIG—
SO WE SENT HER OFF THAT WAY.
"WELL, SHE FOUND IT ALL RIGHT—"
"AND SHE DROVE IT RIGHT AT US!"
"I GUESS SHE WAS MAD 'CAUSE WE'D SENT HER AWAY!"
"BUT THINGS DIDN'T WORK OUT THE WAY SHE'D PLANNED—"
"—'CAUSE IT TURNED AND GRABBED HER—"
"AND COMPLETELY FRIED HER!"
"YEAH, SHE WAS DEAD BEFORE SHE KNEW IT. WHOOSH!"
"SERVES HER RIGHT FOR TRYING TO KILL US, I SAY!"

DEAD!
OH NO.
NO!
YOU SAY SHE DROVE THIS CLANK STRAIGHT AT YOU.
THAT'S A PRETTY ROTTEN THING TO DO.
OH, YEAH! WELL, WE'RE LUCKY OUR PLAN WORKED SO WELL!
WHO KNOWS WHAT SHE WOULD HAVE DONE IF WE'D LET HER STAY!
YOU JUST CAN'T TRUST THAT KIND, I SAY!
SO—UM—WAS THERE A REWARD?
FOR SENDING HER TO HER DEATH?!
A REWARD?!
clic-k
whreee!
AND YOU'RE TELLING ME THAT SHE PURPOSEFULLY SET SOME KIND OF MONSTER ON A GROUP OF HELPLESS PEOPLE?
YOU'RE LYING!
EEK!

NEVER HAVE DONE THAT!

WHERE IS SHE?!

I— I— AH—

STOP THIS!

LISTEN TO ME!

THAT ISN'T WHAT HAPPENED!

WHO GAVE YOU PERMISSION TO—

SHUT UP!

THESE ARE THE WASTELANDS!

WE HAVE TO BE WARY, OR WE'LL BE DEAD!

ABNER—HE WAS GONNA GIVE ME A REWARD!

SHUT UP!

"YES, WE MET HER, AND YES, WE SENT HER AWAY."
"FRANKLY, SHE SCARED THE HELL OUT OF US."
"BUT THE ATTACK BY THE CLANK HAD NOTHING TO DO WITH HER."

"SHE WENT EAST—"
"—IT CAME FROM THE NORTH."

"IT JUST
RIPPED INTO
US."
"BUT
SHE—SHE CAME
BACK AND
STOPPED IT!"
"SHE DIED
SAVING
US."
PIX HERE IS TRYING TO TAKE CREDIT FOR SOMETHING THAT JUST HAPPENED—
—BECAUSE SHE KNOWS YOU'RE LOOKING FOR THIS PERSON—
—AND SHE'S DUMB AND SCARED AND HOPING FOR A REWARD.
PRETTY COLD, AFTER THE GIRL SAVED YOU.
THESE ARE CIRCUS PEOPLE!
GRIFTING IS HOW THEY SURVIVE.
BUT SHE DID SAVE US—
—AND WE BURIED HER LIKE ONE OF OUR OWN.
I DON'T WANT TO BELIEVE EITHER OF YOU.
BUT YOUR STORY—
—IT'S WHAT SHE WOULD HAVE DONE.
YOU'LL SHOW ME THE PLACE YOU SAY THIS HAPPENED.
AND IF YOU'RE PLAYING ME FALSE—
—IF YOU PEOPLE DID DO SOMETHING TO HER—
—I'LL GIVE YOU TO DuPREE—ALONG WITH EVERYONE HERE.
REALLY?!
HONEST?!
OH, YES.

WELL, YOU HEARD THE CRANKY MAN, PAL. LET'S GO.
AND DON'T WORRY, GIRLIE—
IF YOUR BOYFRIEND'S TELLING THE TRUTH—
I'LL MOST LIKELY HAVE TO BRING HIM BACK IN ONE PIECE.
UM—I'M NOT HER—
ABNER—SHUT UP!
YOU'D BETTER COME BACK IN ONE PIECE!
OR I'LL COME AND FIND YOU!
IDIOT!
AB—HERE'S AN EMERGENCY PACK.
JUST IN CASE.
HOKA HEY! WE'RE STILL ALIVE!
NOW WHAT?
NOW I WANT US PACKED AND ON THE ROAD IN TEN MINUTES.
WHAT? BUT IT'S DARK! WE JUST GOT HERE!
LARS—I WANT US GONE—
—BEFORE THE TOWNSFOLK REALIZE THAT WE BROUGHT THEM HERE.
...WE'LL BE READY IN FIVE.

—AND WE...UM...WE PLANTED A *TREE*—
—BECAUSE WE THOUGHT SHE'D...
YOU KNOW... ER...

DIG IT UP.
HA! WHAT'S THE MATTER?
DIDN'T THINK WE'D DO *THAT,* DID YOU?
WHAT!?
MAYBE I'LL GET TO KILL YOU *AFTER*

HOLD IT!
THERE SHE IS!

DAMN! YOU CAN'T BEAT HOME COOKING!
STOP IT.
THAT... COULD BE *ANYBODY.*

FEMALE, YOUNG ADULT, CAUCASIAN, GLASSES.
THESE ARE *HER* CLOTHES AND—

"WHOO— MESSY!
'S GOT THE WULFENBAC SIGIL ON IT.
"RECOGNIZE IT?"

YES. IT'S HERS.
THAT'S HER.
GREAT! CLANK—GET ME A COFFIN!

WHAT ARE YOU DOING *NOW?*
DON'T BE *RIDICULOUS.* THERE'S *NOTHING—*
WELL, I'M *NOT* CARRYING HER IN MY *LAP.*
LISTEN. YOUR FATHER TOLD ME TO BRING HER BACK.
HERE SHE IS—BACK SHE COMES.
ARGUE WITH *HIM.*

WHY *BOTHER?*

ABNER— I'VE SEEN ENOUGH.
I'M INCLINED TO BELIEVE YOUR STORY.
WE'LL TAKE YOU BACK ONCE WE'RE DONE HERE.
ACTUALLY, SIR, I'D RATHER JUST HEAD BACK ON MY OWN.
WHAT?! ACROSS THE WASTE-LANDS?!
WELL, I SHOULD BE OKAY IF I'M CAREFUL AND KEEP TO THE MAIN ROAD.
AND MISS DuPREE THERE—SHE REALLY SCARES ME.
FAIR ENOUGH. SHE'S A SCARY GIRL.
YOU CAN GO.
PLEASE CONVEY MY APOLOGIES TO YOUR SWEETHEART.
I'M AFRAID I GOT RATHER... UPSET.
UM—SIR— I'M SO SORRY ABOUT ALL THIS.
THIS GIRL—IT'S OBVIOUS SHE WAS VERY SPECIAL TO YOU.
SPECIAL?
YES, SHE MIGHT HAVE BEEN...
IT MIGHT HAVE BEEN...
BUT IT ISN'T.
JUST GO.
UM—
YES SIR.

I CAN'T *BELIEVE* ABNER CUT IN ON MY *SCENE* SO *SOON!*
I HAD A *LOT* MORE MATERIAL READY!
FRANKLY, I THINK THE TWO OF YOU WORKED *VERY WELL* TOGETHER.
WELL, *YES,* BUT IF HE'D JUST LET ME KEEP *GOING* A LITTLE *LONGER*—
—THEY PROBABLY WOULDN'T HAVE *TAKEN* HIM!
WHAT WAS HE *THINKING?!*
I'D ASK HIM WHEN HE GETS BACK.
HE'D *BETTER.*
WELL, THAT'S THAT.
COME ON, DEAR—IT'S TIME TO GO.
YES. I GUESS SO.

I STILL CAN'T BELIEVE IT WORKED.
I WAS SO WORRIED.
YOU'D BETTER LEAVE THOSE OFF A WHILE LONGER—
—JUST IN CASE.
OH. RIGHT. SORRY.
PIX WAS AMAZING—
—A PERFECT XENOPHOBIC PEASANT.
BUT—THE PEOPLE THEY SENT—
—IT WASN'T WHAT I EXPECTED.
I HOPE ABNER WILL BE ALL RIGHT.
"ABNER OWES YOU A FAVOR. WE ALL DO."
"THAT CLANK THAT KILLED OLGA—"
"—IT DAMAGED SEVERAL CARTS BEFORE SHE AND ANDRE LED IT OFF."
"I'VE NO DOUBT IT WOULD HAVE COME BACK AFTER IT FINISHED THEM OFF."
YOU SAVED OUR LIVES AND TRIED TO SAVE OLGA'S—
—EVEN AFTER WE SENT YOU AWAY.
WE HAD TO DO THIS.
ANYWAY, ABNER'S A PRO. HE'LL BE FINE.
HE'S PROBABLY GOT THEM CONVINCED YOU NEVER EXISTED BY NOW.
BUT— DRESSING HER IN MY THINGS— DOCTORING THE BODY—
—I DIDN'T WANT TO BE CAUGHT, BUT—
—IT STILL SEEMS DISRESPECTFUL. I'M SORRY.
OLGA WAS WITH US FOR OVER FIVE YEARS.
SHE WAS A GOOD FRIEND AND I KNEW HER VERY WELL.
THIS LIFE—TRAVELING AND PERFORMING— IT WAS EVERYTHING TO HER.

"OLGA WAS NEVER HAPPIER THAN WHEN SHE'D PULLED A REALLY CLEVER SCAM—OR CONVINCED SOME TOWNIE THAT SHE WAS A CONSTRUCT—"
SEE A CONSTRUC ANIMATED BY
"—OR A GRAND DUCHESS, OR AN EXPLORER FROM THE MOON. SHE LOVED THAT SORT OF THING."
AND NOW? NOW SHE GETS TO FOOL NOT JUST SOME GULLIBLE TOWNIE—
—BUT BARON WULFENBACH HIMSELF!
IF SHE WEREN'T DEAD,
SHE'D HAVE KILLED HERSELF TO PLAY THIS PART.
SHOW PEOPLE ARE VERY STRANGE.
YOU'LL GET USED TO IT.
THAT'S WHAT WORRIES ME.
SO THAT WAS ACTING, WAS IT?
IT'S STUPID. YOU STILL SMELLED THE SAME.
I DON'T THINK HE NOTICED.
WELL— HE'S AN IDIOT.

SO... WHAT'S PROFESSOR MOONSOCK GOING TO DO WITH YOU?
THE ANIMAL TRAINER?
WELL, I PROMISED TO HUNT HER UP SOME FRESH MIMMOTHS.
SHE SAYS "OKAY, SO YOU CAN TALK. SO WHAT?"
SHE WANTS TO TEACH ME TO DO A "REAL" ACT.
THAT SOUNDS GREAT!
OH, RIGHT. LIKE SHE CAN TRAIN ME.
OH. SO YOU WON'T DO IT?
OF COURSE I'LL DO IT!
SHE'S GOT CREAM!
I JUST DON'T WANT HER TO THINK IT'LL BE EASY.
RIGHT.
HMF. YOU SMELL KIND OF SAD.
THIS ISN'T ABOUT THAT STUPID WULFENBACH BOY, IS IT?
NO! NO— I JUST FEEL... ODD.
HE— THEY THINK I'M DEAD.
IT'S HARD TO BELIEVE IT'S

DON'T BE A *FOOL.*
RRRAOW!
ZEETHA! I DIDN'T HEAR YOU!
I SHOULD HOPE *NOT!*
I DIDN'T HEAR YOU*!*
GOOD.
SE YOU
I NEVER GOT A CHANCE TO THANK YOU—
—OR TO *APOLOGIZE* FOR MY EARLIER OUTBURST.
THAT'S OKAY. TO LOSE EVERYONE—IT'S *AWFUL.*
NOT SO AWFUL *NOW.*
OH?
AGATHA— I HAVE BEEN WANDERING FOR THREE YEARS NOW—
—AND YOU ARE THE FIRST PERSON WHO HAS EVER *HEARD* OF SKIFANDER.
I WAS BEGINNING TO THINK THAT I HA *MADE IT ALL UP* WHILE I WAS *FEVERISH.*
YOU LET ME KNOW THAT M HOME—
—MY FAMILY—*DOES* EXIST.

FOR THAT, I WISH TO THANK YOU.
OH, WELL— I—
BY STARTING YOU ON WARRIOR TRAINING!
TOMORROW MORNING!
"IT'S OVER."
YOU TALK LIKE A CHILD.
THEY'LL BE BACK—
—AND YOU MUST BE READY.
BUT WHAT MAKES YOU SAY THAT?
IT'S A PERFECT PLAN!
THEY DO THINK I'M DEAD!
THERE IS A SERIOUS FLAW IN THIS "PERFECT PLAN"—
ONE THAT COULD RUIN EVERYTHING.
YOU'RE NOT REALLY DEAD.
NOW ARE YOU?
AH.
TOMORROW MORNING.

BACK ON *CASTLE WULFENBACH*—
DuPREE.
WHEN I SAY THE WORDS *"ALIVE AND UNHARMED"*—
—DO *ANY* NEURONS ACTUALLY *FIRE* IN THAT BRAIN OF YOURS?
UM— NO SIR!
I THOUGHT NOT.
BUT I CAN'T TAKE CREDIT FOR THIS ONE.
SOME OLD SPIDER CLANK BURNED HER DOWN BEFORE WE GOT TO HER.
I SAVED YOU THE SIGIL PLATE.

YES, I SEE.
ONE OF VON BODE'S LITTLE TOYS.
WAS MY SON... UPSET?
<snort> OH, HIM? *YEAH!*
HE'S ALL SET TO BE A HERO AND *RESCUE* HER—
—AND THEN HE FINDS OUT HE'D NEED FIREPLACE TONGS TO GET HER UNDRESSED?
YEAH— UPSET IS THE WORD.
THANK YOU, DuPREE, FOR THAT... VIVID IMAGERY.
YOU MAY GO.
WELL, LET ME KNOW WHEN YOU'VE GOT SOMETHING ELSE FOR ME—
—AND TRY TO MAKE IT ANOTHER *FUN ONE!*
HERR BARON? THE JÄGERGENERALS ARE HERE.
AH—GENERALS. I WANTED TO THANK YOU FOR YOUR RECENT EFFORTS.
YOU IZ VELCOME, HERR BARON.
AND—OH YES—
YOU HAVE BEEN INQUIRING AFTER A...*MISS CLAY?*
VAT? AH, VELL, VE VAS JUST—
YAS. VE DID.
VY?

I AM SORRY TO HAVE TO TELL YOU THAT SHE IS DEAD.
SHE RAN AFOUL OF SOMETHING IN THE WASTELANDS.
I AM NOT HAPPY ABOUT THIS—
—THIS IS *NOT* WHAT I WANTED.
BUT—
DIS IZ—
UF COURZE NOT. WHO VOULD VANT SUCH A TING?
YEZ.
DIS IZ VERY SAD.
SHE VAS A VERY NIZE GIRL.
SAD.
VE GO NOW.
I DON'T **UNDERSTAND** IT.
DuPREE SAW HER **ALIVE.**
WAS IT **REALLY** HER?
WITH MY **SON?**
WHAT WERE THEY **DOING?**
pft. SHE'S A **HETERODYNE.**
AND LUCREZIA'S GIRL.
IT COULD BE **ANYTHING.**
IT'S A PITY SHE'S **DEAD**—
—SHE WOULD HAVE BEEN SO **USEFUL.**
I WONDER...

Z
Z
BEEP!
ZEETHA—
'HAT'S GOING
ON?
REMEMBER? YOU START YOUR WARRIOR TRAINING TODAY.
THIS OUTFIT—
A CLOSE APPROXIMATION OF THE TRADITIONAL NOVICE GARB.
KINDA
CHILLY. ISN'T IT
BIT EARLY FOR
THIS?
MY CONCERN IS THAT I MAY BE TOO LATE.
KNOW, AGATHA CLAY, THAT THE WARRIOR TRADITION OF THE ROYAL HOUSE OF SKIFANDER IS OLD, PROUD AND JEALOUSLY GUARDED.
IN THIS LIFE I AM ALLOWED TO TRAIN ONE OTHER BESIDES MY OWN DAUGHTERS.
I HAVE CHOSEN YOU.
THE BOND BETWEEN US WILL BE STRONGER THAN THAT OF FRIENDS—
—OF FAMILY—
—OF LOVERS.
AS OF NOW, WE ARE "KOLEE-DOK-ZUMIL."
WHAT DOES THAT MEAN?

AH—KIND OF HARD TO TRANSLATE.
SORT OF LIKE "TEACHER AND STUDENT."
SORT OF LIKE "CAUSE AND EFFECT."
MOSTLY, LIKE "GRINDSTONE AND KNIFE."
WHACK!
NOT GOOD.
SO TRY TO STOP ME.
AFTER AN HOUR OF SUCH HILARITY—
PATHETIC.
NO STAMINA.
YOU CAN'T DODGE.
YOU CAN'T BLOCK.
YOU ALLOW ANGER TO DRIVE YOUR ATTACKS—
—AND YOU CAN'T EVEN RUN AWAY PROPERLY.
AND A POOR ATTITUDE.
LUCKY FOR YOU, I LIKE A CHALLENGE!
POKE POKE
SO...THIS DEATH THING THAT THIS IS SUPPOSED TO PREVENT—
—WHY IS IT BAD?
THIS IS LUCKY?
SURE! NOTHING'S BROKEN, IS IT?
I'LL GET YOU SOME BREAKFAST.
A GOOD FIRST DAY.
HOW'D IT GO?

KROSP! HELP! SHE'S GOING TO KILL ME!
IT SOUNDS LIKE SHE'S GOING TO TOUGHEN YOU UP.
GOOD!
THESE ARE THE WASTELANDS!
YOU'VE GOT TO BE TOUGH!
YOU'VE GOT TO BE QUICK!
THAT'S IMPORTANT ENOUGH THAT YOU'VE GOT TO MAKE SACRIFICES.
GOSH. I—
AND TOMORROW, BE A LITTLE MORE CAREFUL.
YOU ALMOST WOKE ME UP.
DIE- THING OF EVIL!
HEY! YOU'RE MOVING!
I'M PRESSED!
WHAT? NO! I—
THE POINT OF THE FIRST DAY IS TO DRIVE YOU TO YOUR ABSOLUTE LIMIT!
YOU'RE NOT AS WEAK AS I THOUGHT!
NO! I AM! I—
SMACK!
GOOD! YOU'RE SNEAKY! I ADMIRE THAT!
AIEEEE!
WHAM!
AAAHH!
MMM! SHE'LL BE SORRY SHE MISSED THIS!

LATER—
AH—THERE YOU ARE, AGATHA. COME ALONG.
OH, NO YOU DON'T. I'M NOT MOVING.
NOW, NOW. EMBI NEEDS AN ASSISTANT.
LET'S GET YOU DRESSED.
SOON—
WHO'S EMBI?
tch.
WE'VE KEPT YOU SO BUSY THE LAST FEW DAYS—
—YOU HAVEN'T HAD A CHANCE TO MEET EVERYONE.
COME WITH ME. IT'S TIME YOU EXPERIENCED SOME THE GLAMOUR AND EXCITEMENT OF SHO BUSINESS.
AAAND—THIS BATCH OF GLAMOUR HERE!
THAT'S A FINE HAT.
THE LATEST FASHION FROM PARIS?
HO! A COMMON MISTAKE.
BUT IT IS A STYLE THAT WAS POPULAR IN MY YOUTH—
—IN A TOWN IN AFRICA THAT YOU'LL HAVE NEVER HEARD OF.
REALLY! THEN YOU'RE A LONG WAY FROM HOME.
VERILY! AM AN EXPLORE
I TRAVEL THESE SAVAGE LANDS IN SEARCH OF THE RARE AND EXOTIC!
EUROPE? SAVAGE? EXOTIC? I NEVER THOUGHT OF US AS UNCIVILIZED...
YOU KNOW, THAT'S WHAT I ALWAYS USED TO SAY TO VISITORS TO MY LAND!
HA! SO WHY ARE YOU WITH THE SHOW?
THE SAME AS YOU. IT IS A FINE WAY TO TRAVEL THROUGH THESE INHOSPITABLE LANDS.
INHOSPITABLE I'LL GRANT YOU.
WHAT'S YOUR ACT?
SOME MUSIC, SOME SLEIGHT-OF-HAND, SOME STORYTELLING...
MOSTLY, I AM SHORT.

IS EVERYONE SHORT WHERE YOU COME FROM?
MY!
INDEED! WHY, WHEN I LEFT HOME, MY NEWEST NEPHEW WAS THE SIZE OF THIS BEET.
<sigh> HE'D BE A GREAT-GREAT GRANDFATHER NOW, I TRUST.
WHAT! HOW OLD ARE YOU?
MMM—I AM NOT SURE, BUT 130 AT LEAST.
IS THAT NORMAL FOR YOUR PEOPLE?
HEAVENS, NO!
"WHEN I WAS YOUNG AND RASH, I MADE A SACRED VOW—"
"—TO SEE THE WORLD BEFORE I DIED."
FRANKLY, I DIDN'T KNOW HOW BIG IT WAS AT THE TIME.
...
BUT WHAT HAS THAT GOT TO DO WITH YOUR LONG LIFE?
ONE OF THE PROBLEMS WITH PEOPLE HERE—
—IS THAT THEY DO NOT TAKE SACRED VOWS AT ALL SERIOUSLY!

SO, MY DEAR, WHAT DO YOU THINK?
IT'S TOO SOON TO TELL.
SHE SEEMS VERY NICE.
BRAVE AND GOOD-HEARTED, TOO.
BUT THEN, *THAT'S* NOT THE QUESTION, *IS* IT?
WE MAY HAVE NOTHING TO FEAR.
WE'LL ONLY TAKE THREE MONTHS OR SO TO GET TO MECHANICSBURG—
IF SHE LEAVES US THERE, SHE MIGHT NEVER EVEN NOTICE ANYTHING.
ARE YOU WORRIED?
MOXANA HAS STARTED A NEW GAME.
WHAT?! *STARTED OVER?* WHY DIDN'T SHE JUST *ADD* HER, LIKE SHE *ALWAYS* DOES?
I...DON'T KNOW.
BUT WHICH PIECE—
NOT JUST A NEW PIECE. A *COMPLETELY NEW GAME.*
WITH COMPLETELY NEW RULES.
I'M STILL WORKING IT ALL OUT—
—BUT THIS MISS CLAY IS THE *CENTER* OF THE *WHOLE THING.*
GOOD LORD.
WHAT *IS* SHE? WHAT HAVE WE *DONE?*
WE DID WHAT WE HAD TO. YOU SAID YOURSELF, WE COULDN'T *LEAVE* HER.
OF *COURSE* NOT. BUT NOW I *AM* WORRIED.
...A *NEW GAME.*
AS AM I.
WELL, *THAT* WAS INTERESTING

I GOT WOOD!
HI MR. EMBI! HI MISS AGATHA!
HELLO, BALTHAZAR!
ONE MORE LOAD AND YOU'RE DONE FOR THE DAY, LADS.
AND IT LOOKS LIKE *YOU'RE* DONE NOW, AGATHA. THANK YOU.
CLANK CLANK
SO WHERE DID YOUR FAMILY GET THIS CLANK?
DAD WAS A SMITH FOR THE GILDED DUKE.
AFTER BARON WULFENBACH BEAT HIM—
—DAD TOOK SMILIN' STEV HERE AS HIS BACK PAY.
HE'S PRETTY SIMPLE.
JUST PULLS OUR CART AND FETCHES WOOD AND WATER.
SEE, THAT'S WHAT CONFUSES ME.
CLANK CLANK CLANK
HUH?
THESE JOINTS ARE SO COMPLEX.
I'D HAVE SWORN THAT THIS WAS A MUCH MORE SOPHISTICATED MECHANISM.
REALLY?
WELL, DADDY SAYS STEV IS BIG AND SLOW AND STUPID—
—JUST LIKE MAMA LIKES 'EM.
WHAT?!
DADDY PLAYS PUNCH A LOT.
OH. RIGHT.

HEY, AGATHA! FEELING BORED?
um—THIS DOESN'T INVOLVE ROOT VEGETABLES, DOES IT?
HARDLY.
OR HITTING ME WITH STICKS...?
NO NO NO.
I THINK YOU KNOW—I AM THE TROUPE'S MUSIC MASTER.
DID I HEAR YOU TELLING MASTER PAYNE YOU COULD PLAY PIANO?
WHY, YES! MY...MOTHER GAVE LESSONS!
GOOOOD!
AND YOU'RE A MECHANIC!
PERFECT!
WE HAVE A REPAIR JOB FOR YOU!
WHEN THAT CLANK ATTACKED, IT COMPLETELY SMASHED OU CALLIOPE.
BEHOLD—THE SILVERODEON!
ONCE THE FINEST MUSIC MACHINE THIS SIDE OF THE CARPATHIANS.
NOW IT'S ONE HUGE MESS—AND IT'S ALL YOURS!
YOU'VE GOT TO BE JOKING! THIS THING IS A DISASTER!
BUT WE'RE ALL SO FOND OF IT. COULDN'T YOU TRY?
WITH WHAT?! CART REPAIR TOOLS?!

OH HO! TOOLS I'VE GOT! COME ON!
CAN'T YOU FIX IT?
AH. WHILE I KNOW KEYBOARDS, I AM, ALAS, NO MECHANIC.
RIVET HERE IS A FINE MECHANIC, BUT DOES NOT PLAY.
BRACE YOURSELF!
sweet lightning!
THEY'RE ALL MINE! THAT'S WHAT I DO!
BUT THIS IS AMAZING!
THE UNIVERSITY DIDN'T HAVE SOME OF THESE!
AND THEY'RE BEAUTIFULLY MADE!
ahem.
YEAH. ...FIND STUFF.
AND REPAIR IT.
WELL! WITH TOOLS LIKE THESE, I SHOULD BE ABLE TO DO SOMETHING!
WONDERFUL!
WHAT IS MASTER PAYNE THINKING?
THAT OLD CALLIOPE IS JUNK!
ALWAYS WAS.
HE SAID TO KEEP HER BUSY. VOILÀ. IT'S DONE.
BUT MY TOOLS!
BETTER YOUR TOOLS THAN YOUR NECK.

HELLO THE CAMP!
AB'S BACK!
BALTHAZAR! TELL MASTER PAYNE!
HEY! THAT WAS QUICK!
THANK THIS FINE HORSE!
WULFENBACH GIVE HIM TO YOU?
HA! I'M NOT THAT GOOD!
I FOUND HIM WANDERING NEAR A CAMPSITE THAT HAD BEEN ATTACKED BY SOMETHING.
ATTACKED BY SOMETHING? IT COULD HAVE STILL BEEN AROUND!
IT COULD HAVE FOLLOWED YOU!

HEY, THERE'S ALWAYS SOMETHING OUT THERE.
GIVE ME SOME CREDIT.
I RODE DOWNSTREAM FOR ABOUT TWO KILOMETERS.
SORRY, AB—IT'S MY JOB.
HE LOOKS PRETTY HUNGRY TO ME.
YEAH—WE'LL FATTEN HIM UP BEFORE HE PULLS ANYTHING.
C'MON LET'S SEE THOSE TEETH!
UMF! CLOSEMOUTHED BEAST!
ABNER!
PIX.
ARE...ARE YOU ALL RIGHT?
I AM.
WELL...WELL GOOD. SO—UM—
SO—
—SO WHAT'S THE IDEA OF HORNING IN ON MY ACT, HEY?
I HAD TO!
I THOUGHT HE WAS GOING TO KILL YOU!
OH NO—I DON'T THINK SO.
HE DIDN'T STRIKE ME AS THE TYPE TO SHOOT AN UNARMED GIRL.
HE WAS JUST MAKING A LOT OF NOISE. I HAD HIM PRETTY RATTLED, AFTER ALL.
BUT IT WOULD HAVE HELPED TO HAVE KNOWN—
—THAT IT WAS A LOVER COMING AFTER YOU, AGATHA.
BUT I—HE'S NOT—
WE ALL THOUGHT THEY WERE LOOKING FOR YOU BECAUSE YOU'D STOLEN SOMETHING!

IT'S ALL RIGHT.
RETICENCE IS TO BE EXPECTED—
—NO DOUBT HE TOOK SHOCKING LIBERTIES.
OH, YES! THAT KIND ALWAYS DOES!
NO DOUBT HE DID TERRIBLE, VILE
YOU POOR GIRL. YOU MUST TELL US ALL ABOUT IT!
NOW WAIT A MINUTE!
SHE ALMOST RAN RIGHT OUT TO HIM.
I EVEN HAD TO HOLD HER BACK FOR A MINUTE THERE
THAT'S BECAUSE I THOUGHT HE WAS GOING TO SHOOT PIX!
OH, OF COURSE.
WELL, DON'T WORRY. I'VE GOT SOMETHING THAT'LL TAKE YOUR MIND OFF HIM.
MORE TRAINING!
THWACK!
NOW, RUN!
NOOOOO!
BAFF!
OUCH.
CRASH!
ERG. YEAH.
SO, PIX. I SEEM TO REMEMBER THIS KISS.
OH, YOU SEEM TO, DO YOU?
WELL, I DON'T THINK I'LL EVER FORGET IT.
OH.
LET'S TALK.
YES.

ATER—

FOUND HER!

HIDING.

HAVE PITY, WHOEVER YOU ARE.

I'M LARS.

I'M ONE OF THE SHOW'S ADVANCE MEN.

MOST OF THE TIME, I'M NOT EVEN HERE!

WHEN YOU GO, TAKE ME WITH YOU!

HO! USUALLY WE GET FARM GIRLS WHO WANT TO *JOIN* THE SHOW TO ESCAPE!

ESCAPE— FROM WHAT?

H—THE EDIUM OF ARMING,
THE DULL LAD THEY'RE DOOMED TO MARRY,
A TOWN THAT REMEMBERS OUR MISTAKES.
GOSH. WHAT DO YOU DO WITH THEM?
WHY, WE AKE THEM, OF COURSE!
YOU DO?

SURE! IF THEY DON'T PANIC THEIR FIRST NIGHT AWAY FROM HOME— THEY USUALLY LEAVE AT THE NEXT TOWN.
BUT SOME—
—AH, SOME SET FOOT ON THE STAGE AND NEVER STEP OFF.
LIKE YOURSELF?
HA! CAUGHT!

"INDEED, YOU SEE BEFORE YOU A FORMER CHEESEMAKER'S APPRENTICE—"
"WHO STOPPED TO SEE A TRAVELING HETERODYNE SHOW."

REALLY!
OH YES! IT WAS THE HETERODYNE BOYS AND THE MYSTERY OF THE CAST IRON GLACIER.
THAT WAS OVER TEN YEARS AGO AND I'VE NEVER REGRETTED IT.
MY FAVORITE WAS ALWAYS "RACE TO THE WEST POLE."
OH, YEAH, WE HAVEN'T DONE THAT ONE IN A WHILE.
THAT'S TOO BAD. WHY NOT?
OH, I DON'T KNOW. THERE'S SO MANY OF THEM, YOU KNOW—
—WE JUST HAVEN'T GOTTEN AROUND TO IT IN A WHILE, I GUESS.
AND THERE'S SOME TOUGH SCENES IN WEST POLE.
REMEMBER THE SCENE ON THE BURNING SUBMARINE?
"RENOUNCE YOUR FATHER LEST HIS EVIL CORRUPT YOU!"
OH, YES. WAIT—AH—
"ONE CANNOT BE CORRUPTED BY SCIENCE, AND SCIENCE ALONE IS MY MASTER!"
"THEN YOUR MASTER IS MAD! AS MAD AS YOU HAVE DRIVEN ME!"
"IS IT MADNESS TO SEE CLEARLY?"
"YOU ONLY CONFUSE ME!"
"ALLOW ME TO ELUCIDATE!"
"...IT COULD BE AN INTERESTING EXPERIMENT—
"—IF I BUT DARED..."
"I FEAR THE RESULT—BUT THE EXPERIMENT ITSELF—"
"—WHY—THAT IS SCIENCE!"
"DON'T TELL ME YOU FEAR THE EXPERIMENT?!"
"FOR SCIENCE, THEN."
"FOR SCIENCE!"

SAY! YOU'RE PRETTY GOOD!
REALLY? I NEVER... I MEAN...
SO THAT'S ACTING?
TWERLIK?
LARS?
shhhhh!
SU FIG?
—geisterdamen.

KLIBBER MEENAK SEG NI PLOSTOK VEDIK KLIZ MOC TWERLIK?
ZO—ZO FLOODA VEDIK.
BOTCHA HEY ZA VEDIK MOC, NODOK.
ZA NIKTIK EVE ZA GWOON.
HIC MOC?!
ZO—VOCO CHEEB?
KLOOPA.
OBONGS.
SET VE?
ZA "ACTORS."
"ACTORS?!
WOGE-ZE FLEEPIN BO "ACTORS," BIN?
YAN DOH IP ZA CHEEB.
HIF NI!

I...I DIDN'T VEN HEAR THEM COMING.
WHO *ARE* THEY?
THEY CALL 'EM GEISTERDAMEN. WEIBDAMEN. SPIDER RIDERS.
ALL KINDS OF THINGS.

THEY'VE BEEN AROUND FOR YEARS.
THEY'RE ALWAYS ON THE MOVE.
NOBODY KNOWS ANYTHING ABOUT THEM, REALLY.
EXCEPT—YOU *DON'T* WANT TO FIGHT THEM.
FARMERS SAY THEY CAUSE REVENANTS—
STEAL CHILDREN—
BLIGHT CROPS—
—THE USUAL. BRRR.
I'VE NEVER *HEARD* OF THEM.

LOTS OF THINGS YOU VER HEAR ABOUT OUTSIDE THE WASTELANDS.
SO—
WANT TO GET DROPPED OFF AT THE NEAREST TOWN?
NO, THANKS.
HEY!
YOU TWO OKAY?

SORRY, AGATHA, BUT AS NEW KID, YOU GET OL' BABA YAGA HERE.
DRIVING HER'S A BEAR.
SHE'S A DOUBLE-CLUTCH BELGIAN OVERGEAR SNAP POSITION SYSTEM—
YOU'LL GET IT IN A MONTH OR TWO.
BABA YAGA
THERE'S NO GYROS OR SHOCK ABSORBERS TO SPEAK OF—
—SHE TURNS LIKE A COW—
—AND YOU'LL HAVE TO STOP EVERY FIFTEEN MINUTES TO REFUEL THE BOILER.
PLUS, THE ROOF LEAKS, THE LEFT PISTON TENDS TO LOSE PRESSURE SO IT'LL TIP OVER AT NIGHT—
—AND IT'S HAUNTED!
THE GOOD NEWS IS YOU GET TO BUNK SOLO.
SO?
BUT THIS THING IS A WALKING DISASTER AREA!
WHY DO YOU EVEN BOTHER TO KEEP IT RUNNING?
WE NEED THE EGGS.

HAT A
DAY.
I'M EXHAUSTED.
Mph.
HEY, WHAT'S
WRONG?
THERE'S SOMETHING THESE PEOPLE AREN'T TELLING US.
THAT'S NOT SURPRISING.
WE'RE NOT TELLING THEM EVERYTHING ABOUT US.
THAT'S THEIR PROBLEM.
WHAT EXACTLY IS BOTHERING YOU?
THESE PEOPLE HAVE NO WEAPONS.
I'VE BEEN LOOKING AROUND. NOTHING.
UM—THOSE LONG POINTY THINGS ARE CALLED SWORDS.
Pft. REAL WEAPONS.
WHEN THAT SPIDER CLANK ATTACKED, THEY SCATTERED AND RAN!
YES—SO?
SO I'VE READ SOME OF WULFENBACH'S REPORTS.
THAT CLANK WAS NOTHING COMPARED TO SOME OF THE STUFF OUT HERE—
—AND THESE PEOPLE HAVE BEEN TRAVELING AROUND FOR YEARS—ESSENTIALLY UNARMED?
THEY SHOULD BE DEAD!
NO. THEY
MUST HAVE
OMETHING.
THEN WHY DIDN'T THEY USE IT AGAINST THE CLANK?
THE ONLY THING THAT MAKES SENSE IS THAT THEY WERE HIDING IT FROM YOU.
ME?! WHY ME?
I DON'T KNOW.
MAYBE IT'S JUST THAT YOU'RE A STRANGER.
KROSP—THAT THING PICKED OLGA UP AND FRIED HER!
WHAT COULD I DO THAT'S WORSE THAN THAT?
I DON'T KNOW. I'M MISSING SOMETHING.

BIP!
WHERE'D THAT COME FROM?!
IT'S MINE.
I FOUND IT BURIED IN THE PACK.
ITS SPRING HAD RUN DOWN.
hmf. I DON'T LIKE IT.
YOU DON'T HAVE TO.
ANYWAY, IT'S HARMLESS
I HAVE TO WIND IT EVERY DAY OR IT'LL STOP.
PITY IT'S SO USELESS.
NOW THAT GUN—
—THAT WE SHOULD HAVE KEPT.
WE'VE BEEN OVER THAT.
LEAVING IT ON THE GRAVE WAS A MARK OF RESPECT.
ANYWAY, THE BARON'S PEOPLE WOULD NEVER HAVE LET THEM KEEP IT.
YES, YES...
BESIDES, WE DON'T REALLY NEED IT—
—SINCE I'VE ALREADY BUILT TWO BETTER ONES.
YOU'RE WORRIED TOO.
NOT WORRIED...
I JUST HAVE THIS WEIRD FEELING...

"AND IT'S BEEN *ROWING* ALL DAY..."

GOOD NIGHT, LARS.

SLEEPING OUTSIDE, AS USUAL?

OF COURSE. I LIKE FIRST WATCH—

—AND IT'S A *FINE* NIGHT.

IN THE MORNING I'LL PRY AUGIE AWAY FROM WANDA—

—AND WE'LL BE OFF TO THE NEXT TOWN BEFORE DAWN.

WE'LL HAVE THEM ALL READY AND EXPECTING A GRAND SHOW BY THE TIME *YOU* SLOWPOKES GET THERE!

VERY GOOD! FARE THEE WELL, THEN.

SNAP!
WHO'S THERE?

OH FOR—
NOW HOW'D YOU GET LOOSE?
WELL, COME ON, LET'S—

SKREEONK!

SSSSS...
WHAT THE—
HEY!
THUD
THUD
SCREE!
HELP!
HELP!
HA!
CRAK!
UH OH.
!?
EYES!

FOOM!
POW!
POW!
POW!
POW!
POW!
SKRONK!
THAT WAS A *DIRECT HIT*.
DID IT DO *ANYTHING?*
AT! AT! AT! AT! AT!
SCRIEK!!
K-CHAK-PUM
STEV! DESTROY!
YES. IT GOT IT *MAD*.
WHREEE!

PWHAM!
COVER YOUR EARS!
I'M USING THE SONIC GUN!
EEEEE
AUT VINCERE AUT MORI!
chok!
I'M POWERING UP THE GRAVITY ENGINE!
OOOMMMMM
NONE OF THAT IS WORKING!
I'M RELEASING MY POISONOUS SKY WYRMS!
DANGER
NO!
ZZZZZZZZZZZZZZZZ
FWAAAAH!
IT BREATHES FIRE?!
OH! THAT'S CHEATING! IT'S NOT FAI

YAAAA!
FWUMP!
SNAK!
DIE!
AH!
RHAA!
AAAAH!
RHAAAAAAA!
BLAZAPHT!

VREEEEOOOOOEEEE
WELL.
THIS EXPLAINS A LOT.
YOU'RE ALL SPARKS.
AREN'T YOU?

GHAAA!
LARS?
IT'S OKAY! TAKE A DEEP BREATH!
HORSE! HORSEHORSE HORSEHORSE!
WELL, I GUESS THAT'S OVER, THEN.
WHAT IN THE WORLD IS THE MATTER WITH HIM?
PANIC ATTACK.
HE GETS THEM AFTER THINGS LIKE THIS.
HUH. THAT'S KIND OF WEIRD FOR A SPARK, ISN'T IT?
HE'S NOT A SPARK.
WHAT? BUT—
SEVERAL OF US ARE—BUT NOT ALL OF US.
ANOTHER PANIC ATTACK, EH?
GREAT! A CHANCE TO TRY MY CALMING PIE.
HORSE—
SPLAFF!

HORRRFF!
THAT WAS SUPPOSED TO *CALM HIM DOWN?*
THOSE OF US WHO *ARE* SPARKS—
AREN'T NECESSARILY THAT *GOOD* AT IT.
NN...
tch. YOU'VE SPRAINED THAT ANKLE.
WE'LL BIND IT UP AND HAVE YOU STAY OFF IT A FEW DAYS.
AH! A CHANCE TO TRY MY NEW "RELATIVISTIC PA THEORY!"
LET ME GET MY HAMMER.
HUH. ALL THE *CALM* MUST HAVE LEAKED OUT.
I'LL BAKE A *FRESH* ONE.
BOSH! WE SHOULD AMPUTATE-
-AND TRY OU MY NEW STEAM-POWER FEET!
COME *NEAR* ME AND I WILL *KILL* YOU.
FINE. SUFFER, THEN.
YOU KNOW, I BET LARS WOULDN'T PANIC-
-IF HIS FEET COULD RUN AT TWO HUNDRED KILOMETERS PER HOUR.
CAN *I* HAVE THE BODIES WHEN YOU'RE DONE?
ABSURD. THE STRESS WOULD TEAR THE LEGS APART.
AH-OLD FASHIONED FLESH LEGS, YES, BUT-
ENOUGH!
ALL LARS NEEDS IS A LIE-DOWN AND SOME *QUIET!*
YES, COUNTESS.
SORRY, COUNTESS.
AND... AND PERHAPS... A *SOOTHING TONIC?*
YES! WHY DON'T YOU GO BREW ONE UP, DEAR?
MISS CLAY—DO *YOU* HAVE ANY IDEAS FOR CALMING HIM DOWN?
ME? HEAVENS, *NO.*
EXCELLENT. HELP ME GE HIM UP, WON YOU?
HORSE! PIE!
HORSE! PIE!
HORSE! PIE!

DON—
SO THE POINT IS, EVERYBODY KNOWS WHAT THE SPARK IS—RIGHT??
JUST ASK THE PEOPLE WHO COME TO OUR SHOWS.
TO THEM, "THE SPARK" MEANS YOU'RE ANOTHER LIKE WULFENBACH, OR THE HETERODYNES.
SO?
EXCEPT IT DOESN'T ALWAYS WORK LIKE THAT.
"WHAT ABOUT SOMEONE ALLY BRILLIANT, BUT BORN INTO A POOR VILLAGE?"
"WITHOUT ANY EDUCATION, WHAT CAN THEY DO?"
"AND THERE ARE... VARYING DEGREES OF TALENT."
"THE WORST OFF ARE THOSE WITH JUST ENOUGH TALENT THAT PEOPLE SAY 'AH, A SPARK'—
—BUT WITH LITTLE POWER TO PROTECT THEMSELVES."
AT IS WHAT YOU ILL FIND HERE.
WE PLAY MADBOYS ON THE STAGE AND PERFORM MUNDANE MIRACLES."
"WE'RE JUST PLAYERS IN A SHOW, AND SO WE ARE ABLE TO HIDE IN PLAIN SIGHT."
DR. PRONI AND OLLY
"EVEN FROM THE BARON."
YOU THOUGHT HE HAD SENT THE SPIDER CLANK.
THE BARON OR SOMEONE LIKE HIM.
THERE ARE MANY WHO HAVE A USE FOR WEAK SPARKS.
I SEE. WELL, IT'S LATE, I GUESS I'D BETTER GO—
NO!
I WANT HER TO STAY! HER!
MISS CLAY? WHY?

BECAUSE SHE'S GOT A GREAT BIG MONSTER-KILLING GUN—
AND I WANT IT AND HER RIGHT HERE!
I'LL STAY.
CAN'T ARGUE WITH THAT LOGIC.
THANK YOU, MISS CLAY. I APPRECIATE IT.
Z
HEAVENS! HE'S ALREADY ASLEEP.
WELL! NOBODY'S HA THAT MUCH FA IN ME SINCE—
Z
...SINCE?
NOTHING. NEVER MIND.
I SEE. GOOD NIGHT, THEN.
GOOD NIGHT.
IS LARS OKAY, SIR?
MM? OH, YES. MISS CLAY WILL STAY WITH HIM.
HUH. I GUESS THERE'S NO MORE DOUBT—
—SHE'S A SPARK. A STRONG ONE, I'D GUESS.
THAT'S RIGHT.
AND ON THE RUN FROM WULFENBACH.
WELL, MOXANA'S NEW GAME IS MAKING MORE AND MORE SENSE.
YOU DON'T SOUND HAPPY.
WE... COULD LOSE HER AT THE NEXT TOWN...
NO, AB—I DON'T THINK WE COULD.
OUR TASK IS TO GET HER TO MECHANICSBURG.
WE'LL MOVE OUT IN THE MORNING.
USE ALL THE WOOD YOU NEED. I WANT THAT HORSE BURNED TONIGHT.
I'LL DO IT MYSELF.
GOOD LAD.

IDE THE SPARK.
I'VE HEARD THAT BEFORE, BUT IT SEEMS LIKE IT WOULD BE TOUGH.
IT'S EASIER FOR THEM. THEY HAVE LESS TO HIDE.
I CAN STILL LEARN A *LOT* FROM THEM.
uh-huh. THEIR *PROBLEM* IS THEIR VULNERABILITY.
YES—THEY DON'T BUILD ANYTHING VERY POWERFUL—
AND THEY COULDN'T HIDE IT WELL IF THEY *DID*.
BUT I'LL BET *I* COULD...
YESSS— WITH HE TOOLS AND MATERIALS AVAILABLE—
—WHY, I COULD BUILD DEVICES THAT WOULD KEEP US SAFE FROM *ANYONE!*
WITHOUT BEING OBVIOUS?
THEY MIGHT NOT APPRECIATE YOUR TINKERING.
OF COURSE!
WHEN I'M DONE—
—WE WILL BE THE MOST NORMAL LOOKING CIRCUS ON EARTH!
OH GOOD. VERY REASSURING.
LATER—
...AND ANOTHER SET OF BALLISTA... *HERE*.
YES!
DONE!
Z
WHEW.
ERK. (yawn)
DONE?
UH-HUH. WANT TO *SEE?*
A NUTCRACKER? BUT—
AAH!
WHAT?
A MERRY-GO-ROUND THAT CAN LEVEL A SMALL *TOWN*—
—SEEMS A BIT OVERBOARD FOR "SELF-DEFENSE!"
WELL... IT COULD BE A REALLY *EVIL* TOWN...
AGATHA!
OKAY, OKAY.

I DOUBT I'D NEED ANYTHING THIS EXTREME, ANYWAY.
-yawn- I AM SO READY TO—
YOU'RE AWAKE!
EAGER FOR TRAINING, EH?
HA! I'D HEARD SPARKS WERE TOUGH!
WELL! NO MORE MOLLY-CODDLING!
NO...
IS SOMEONE THERE?
WHERE'D AGATHA GO?
OFF TO BED?
I'LL BET SHE WAS PRETTY BEAT.
SHE WILL BE.
HM? WOW— SHE WAS BUSY.
BUT WHAT IS IT?
ER... AH...
HUH. SOME SORT OF CHERRY PITTER...
I THINK...
MMM... IS THAT BREAKFAS I SMELL?
MAN— I SURE HOPE NOT.
MORNIN' LARS. DOESN'T LOOK SO SCARY NOW, DOES HE?
THAT DEPENDS. WHAT'S FOR BREAKFAST?
OATMEAL—
À LA MONSTER!
AH! WELL THEN—
ERG. YOU'RE HORRIBLE.
HEH.
WELL! PIX SURE LOOKS HAPPY.
sh—WE SAT UP ALL NIGHT WATCHING THIS THING BURN.
WHOA! AND I THOUGHT I KNEW HOW TO SHOW A GIRL A GOOD TIME!
WELL, WE HAD A GOOD LON TALK.

JUST ALKED?
JUST TALKED.
hmf. YOU LOOK PRETTY HAPPY FOR A COUPLE WHO "JUST TALKED."
GUESS WE LIKED WHAT WE HEARD.
GOOD MORNING, ALL.
READY TO GO, LARS?
ANYTIME AUGIE'S READY.
EXCELLENT! WE'LL BE RIGHT BEHIND YOU.
SO— NYTHING NUSUAL?
JEWELED HEART?
ENCHANTED PRINCESS?
'FRAID NOT, SIR. IT SMELLED LIKE HORSE.
PITY.
poke poke
WE'LL JUST HAVE TO COME UP WITH SOMETHING INTERESTING URSELVES, THEN.
MAKE A GOOD STORY OUT OF IT.
BAH! NOVICES TODAY!
ASK THEM TO MOVE SOME ROCKS AND THEY JUST COLLAPSE.
WHY, WHEN I TRAINED...
hm. AND I THINK WE'LL HAVE RIVET DRIVE THE BABA YAGA TODAY.
GOOD IDEA, SIR.

(yawn) HELLO, WE'VE MOVED.
WE SURE HAVE!
YOU'VE BEEN ASLEEP ALL DAY!
HO! AGATHA! WE'VE MADE CAMP EARLY TODAY.
WE HIT A STRETCH OF GOOD ROAD—
—AND OL' BABA YAGA HASN'T BROKEN DOWN ONCE!
YEAH! IT'S KIN OF WEIR
IT SURE IS WEIRD. WHAT'D YOU DO WITH IT?
NO BREAKDOWNS, NO JAMMING—
BUT— I—
I'D SWEAR THE GEARAGE IMPROVED WHILE I WAS DRIVING IT.
IT'S AMAZING! YOU'VE GOT TO SHOW ME HOW YOU DID IT!
I HAVEN'T DONE ANYTHING YET!
I MEAN— I LOOKED IT OVER—
—AND I MADE SOME SKETCHES, BUT—
THEN THE HORSE WENT AFTER LARS, AND—
—WELL, I HAVEN'T HAD THE TIME!
NO.
I REFUSE TO BELIEVE THAT YOU'RE SOME KIND OF MAGICAL SPARK—
—WHO CAN FIX SOMETHING JUST BY "MAKING A FEW SKETCHES."
SOMEONE FIXED THAT CART.
AND I'M GONNA FIND OUT HOW!
WELL, I DON'T KNOW!
IT WASN'T ME!

ANWHILE—
IT'S JUST SUCH A WASTE!
A CAT WHO SINGS! DANCES!
BUT... NOT VERY WELL...
HE'S AWFUL!
AND YET, A REAL CAT SINGING AND DANCING—
RROWRRROWRR!
HM. THAT'S THE PROBLEM. HE'S UNMISTAKABLY REAL.
IT MIGHT BE BEST IF WE KEEP HIM OFF THE STAGE ENTIRELY.
WHAT? RIDICULOUS!
YOU CAN'T ALL HAVE TIN EARS!
ANYWAY, YOU PEOPLE ARE HARDLY THE PARIS OPERA.
THIS SHOW NEEDS MY TALENT!
OH, I QUITE AGREE.
ON—
OH! DON'T YOU LOOK ONDERFUL!
THANK YOU.
NO, REALLY!
THE COAT BRINGS OUT YOUR NATURAL LEADERSHIP QUALITIES!
REALLY.
AND IT WAS SO NICE OF THEM TO SAY YOU COULD KEEP IT!
'CAUSE BALTHAZAR OUTGREW IT.
um— AND YOU'RE MAKING A VALUABLE CONTRIBUTION TO—
JUST DROP IT, OKAY?!
HEY, AGATHA!
THEY WANT YOU OVER HERE!

WHAT'S GOING ON?
AND DAME AEDITH WILL DO HER KNIFE THROWING.
THIS TIME, DO *NOT* ASK IF THERE ARE ANY VAMPIRES IN THE AUDIENCE!
HOW WAS *I* TO KNOW THAT GUY WAS *JOKING?*
WHO'D JOKE ABOUT *VAMPIRES?!*
WE'LL BE HITTING THE TOWN OF ZUMZUM SOON.
SO THEY'RE ASSIGNING PARTS FOR THE SHOW.
SO THAT BRINGS US TO THE MAIN SHOW—
—AND THE HETERODYNE PLAY WE'LL BE DOING.
HOW ABOUT *THE FOG MERCHANT?*
I'VE GOT SOME LADDER BUSINESS I WANT TO TRY IN SCENE 2!
OO! OO! *CLOCKWORK SUNDIAL!*
HOW ABOUT *THE RACING SNAILS OF DR. ZEGREB?*
TOO BAD, IT'S ALREADY DECIDED.
WE'RE DOING *RACE TO THE WEST POLE.*
OO— HAVEN'T DONE *THAT* ONE IN A WHILE.
BUT I THOUGHT P DIDN'T LIKE PLAYING LUCREZIA.
I *DON'T.* I ALWAYS WANTED TO PLAY THE *HIGH PRIESTESS.*
WHICH IS WHY *AGATHA* GETS TO PLAY LUCREZIA.
WHAT? BUT—
LARS SAID YOU'RE PRETTY GOOD—
—AND I'VE LEARNED TO TRUST HIS INSTINCTS.
BESIDES, HE PLAYS BILL AND HE'S GOOD AT ONSTAGE COACHING.
HB
RACE TO THE WEST POLE
WEL.

BUT WHAT IF I'M NO GOOD?
WELL— WE'VE FOUND THAT NONE OF THE HETERODYNE PLAYS REALLY SUFFER—
—IF PUNCH AND JUDY START THROWING PIES.
I'M GONNA STUDY MY LINES.
ANOTHER SUCCESS FOR MY UNIFIED PIE THEORY.
YEAH, YEAH, SO PUBLISH, ALREADY.
HERE. YOU'RE KLAUS.
OF COURSE!
"DO NOT TEMPT ME!
YOUR BROTHER APPROACHES, AND I MUST GO!"
um—BLAH BLAH, EXPLODING BANANAS—
—BLAH BLAH, "POLE OF MY HEART—"
ah—THAT WAS YOUR LAST LINE.
GOOD JOB.
WELL—I SAW IT A LOT.
SOMETHING WRONG?
THIS FEELS SO WEIRD...
OH?
WELL, IF I REALLY AM THE DAUGHTER OF BILL AND LUCREZIA HETERODYNE—
—THEN THESE STORIES—
—ALL THE HETERODYNE STORIES—
—ARE ABOUT MY PARENTS.
THIS PART— I'M PLAYING MY OWN MOTHER—
—AND LARS PLAYS MY FATHER!
SO?
SO THERE'S KISSING AND STUFF.
IT FEELS WEIRD.
OH, WELL. WHEN YOU KISS HIM, DON'T THINK OF HIM AS BILL HETERODYNE.
JUST PRETEND HE'S GILGAMESH WULFENBACH.
OR NOT.

A FEW DAYS LATER, IN THE TOWN OF ZUMZUM—
SHE'S GUNNA KEEL US, HYU KNOW.
HY KNOW, HY KNOW.
HO! VE SHOULD GET OFF SO EASY.
HYU GOTS THAT RIGHT.
SHE CAN BE VERY UNREASONABLE.
HEY! VAIT A MINUTE!
MAYBE VE GETS LUCKY!
MEBBE VE BE DEAD BY THE TIME SHE GETS HERE!
OOH! HADN'T THOUGHT OF THAT!
IZ YOU CRAZY? DEN VE REALLY BE IN TROUBLE!
HO— COMPANY!
ARE YOU INSANE?
WE CAN'T PERFORM HERE!
I KNOW SIR— I TRIED.
BUT ALL ENTERTAINME HAS TO BE I THE TOWN SQUARE.
PERFORMING NEXT TO CORPSES IS DISRESPECTFUL—
—AND UNHYGIENIC!
AH—WELL, IF THAT'S THE ONLY PROBLEM—

SORRY FOR DE TROUBLE!
THEY'RE STILL ALIVE?!
THEY'VE BEEN UP FOR TWO DAYS!
THEY JUST AREN'T DYING!
BUT— TRADITIONALLY THEY'RE SUPPOSED TO BE CUT DOWN.
NOT LIKELY. THE MAYOR'S GOT A BETTING POOL GOING.
LOVELY.
OH, HE IS THAT.
HEY! DIS IZ GREAT!
YAH! VE GETS TO SEE A SHOW FOR FREE!
HEY! SHOT UP!
SHOT UP!
USE YOU NOSES!
VHERE IZ IT?
VHERE? HIM? NO—
"DERE!"
HEY, WHAT'S UP?
I DON'T KNOW.
I JUST—
AH! JÄGERKIN!
WHAT?
OH, RIGHT. I HEARD ABOUT THEM.
BAD BUSINESS.

WHAT DID THEY DO?
BE JÄGERMONSTERS AND GET CAPTURED, WHAT ELSE?
OH. BUT—
—WON'T THE BARON BE UPSET?
THE BARON DON'T CARE ABOUT US, MISS.
SERGEANT ZULI, AT YOUR SERVICE.
WE'RE TOO SMALL AND OUT-OF-THE-WAY HERE.
IT'S A RARE EVENT WHEN WE SEE THE BARON'S PATROL SHIPS OVERHEAD.
PLUS, THESE ONES WEREN'T EVEN WEARING HIS BADGE.
THESE ARE WILD JÄGERS.
AND TO THEM WITH LONG MEMORIES—
—THEM WHAT REMEMBERS THE HETERODYNES—
—THAT MAKES THEM FAIR GAME.
THE HETERODYNES! BUT BILL AND BARRY—
BLESS YOU, MISS. OF COURSE THEY WERE THE GOOD ONES.
I MEAN BEFORE THEM.
THE OLD HETERODYNES.
"MURDERIN' DEVILS, EVERY ONE—"
"—AND THE JÄGERS RODE WITH THEM—"
"—KILLIN' FOR SPORT AND LAYING WASTE WHEREVER THEY WENT."
THAT'S WHAT THE OLD FOLKS REMEMBER.
TO THEM, THIS IS JUST THE WHEEL OF JUSTICE GRINDING SLOW BUT FINE.
WELL, GOOD DAY, LADIES.
HEY!
SMAK!
I...I HADN'T... REALLY THOUGHT ABOUT IT.
NOT LIKE THAT.
WELL, YEAH. THE HETERODYNE BOYS REALLY REDEEMED THE FAMILY.
BUT PEOPLE STILL SCARE THEIR KIDS WITH STORIES ABOUT THE JÄGERS.
NOW, THAT'S CREEPY.
WHAT?

I DON'T KNOW WHAT IT IS—
BUT THEY'VE BEEN STARING AT *YOU* NONSTOP.
REALLY? OH—
UH—MAYBE— MAYBE WE SHOULD STAY *AWAY* FROM THEM.
LET'S *GO.*

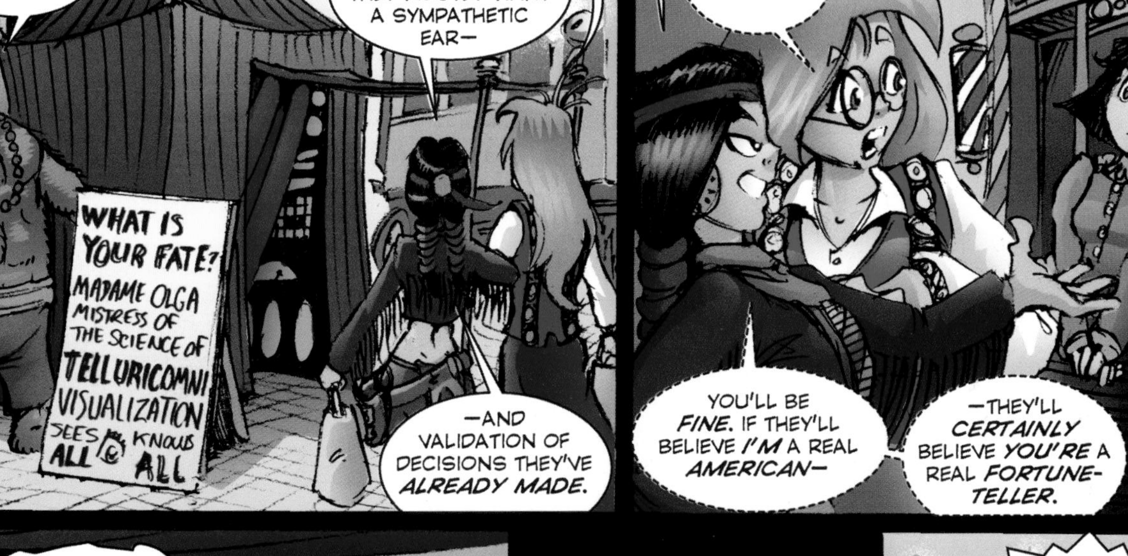

ER—HAVE NO FEAR, MY CHILD.
THE DATA INDICATE THAT ALL WILL BE WELL.
'kay.
SOMETHING WRONG?
SHE...
...TEA COZY...
...FORTY-THREE HOURS...
...ONLY ONE SPOON...
...HOW...
EEK!
WELL, YOU HAVE TO KEEP AN OPEN MIND.
PEOPLE DO ALL SORTS OF THINGS.
IT DOESN'T MAKE THEM BAD.
IT ISN'T THAT.
IT'S JUST...
HOW CAN I ADVISE THEM WHEN I DON'T EVEN UNDERSTAND THE QUESTIONS?
FOR ALL I KNOW, THE TEA COZY THING IS NORMAL HERE.
WELL, USUALLY YOU USE COMMON SENSE, LOGIC—
WHOO! YOU GOT A SPICY ONE, DIDN'CHA?
—AND WHEN NECESSARY, ASK AN EXPERT.
GIMME DETAILS!
YOU'RE AN EXPERT?
HEY, SKIFANDER'S PATRON GODDESS IS ASHTARA.
SHE WHO, AMONG OTHER THINGS, CONTROLS LOOOVE!
OUR HOLY DAYS ARE FUN!
(CHA CHA CHA!)
WELL, I JUST FOUND YOU A NEW BISHOP.
AGATH
HA. YOU'RE JUST STARTING.
TALK TO ME IN A WEEK!
THE SHOW STARTS IN TEN MINUTES!
WE'VE GOT TO GET YOU READY!
BYE, KID! BREAK A LEG!
YEAH, JUST DON'T DANC ON IT!
OW!
I CAN DO THIS—
I CAN DO THIS—

—ON—
YOU'RE ALMOST ON! NERVOUS?
RELAX! IF YOU MESS UP WE'LL COVER FOR YOU!
DADDY! HERE'S MORE PIES!
ONLY BECAUSE PEOPLE KEEP ASKING ME THAT!
NO NO NO!
YOU'RE LUCREZIA MONGFISH!
OKAY. NOW I'M NERVOUS.
YOU'RE MAD!
YOU'RE BAD!
YOU'RE DANGEROUS!
YES! YES!
"I THINK TOO MUCH—
—THEREFORE I AM MAD!"
GRR!
"I PRAY THE MISTRESS IS IN A GOOD MOOD—"
THAT'S YOUR CUE! GO!
OF COURSE I AM!
IT IS A GLORIOUS DAY FOR-
GAK!

FOR SCIENCE!
I... I...
ahem. HAS THE TRAP BEEN SET, MISTRESS?
ah. YES.
YES! AND SOON-
ALL OF THE HETERODYN SECRETS WI BE MINE!
THAT WAS A GREAT FIRST ACT!
VERY EDGY! IT WAS LIKE YOU EXPECTED SOMEONE TO SHOOT YOU!
WAS—WAS THAT OTHAR TRYGGVASSEN OUT THERE?
OH YEAH! HE LOVES OUR SHOWS!
HE'S— YOU'VE ALL MET HIM BEFORE?
HE GETS AROUND A LOT.
WE'VE SEEN HIM FIVE, NO, SIX TIMES IN THE PAST YEAR.
BUYS A LOT OF POPCORN.
AND HE HASN'T SHOT ANYBODY?
OF COURSE NOT. HE GETS FREE REFILLS!
BUT—
"YOU! MINION!"
THERE YOU GO!
BUT—
"WHY AM I TIED TO THIS TABLE?
AND WHERE ARE MY PANTS?"

WHO HAS DEACTIVATED MY BEAUTIFUL FROGS?
HE DID!
AND SO THE SHOW GOES ON—
DON'T TELL ME YOU FEAR THE EXPERIMENT?!
I FEAR THE RESULT-
—TO THE END...
...THERE YOU WILL FIND—
—THE POLE OF MY HEART.
LET'S GO, EVERYBODY! CURTAIN CALL!
HE'S GONE?
CLAP!
CLAP!
CLAP!
CLAP!
CLAP!
CLAP!

HEE HEE! LISTEN TO THEM CHEER!
I KNEW YOU'D BE GREAT!
COME ON! NOW WE MINGLE WITH THE AUDIENCE!
OH, UH—NO,
I'D REALLY RATHER—
EEK!
SO! MADAME OLGA!
SAYER OF SOOTHS AND TELLER OF FORTUNES, YES?
AH—YES?
EXCELLENT! I WOULD LIKE MY FORTUNE TOLD!
NOW.
SEE YOU LATER, OLGA!
SO.
A FINE PERFORMANCE!
THANK YOU.
YOU SEEM ON EDGE.
THE LAST TIME I SAW YOU, YOU TRIED TO SHOOT ME.
OH, THAT!
THAT WAS BEFORE I KNEW YOU WERE A HETERODYNE!
"WHAT?! HOW COULD YOU KNOW THAT?!"
"WHY, NOT LONG AFTER WE PARTED WAYS—"
"—I RAN INTO YOUR COUSIN DuMEDD."
"A NICE YOUNG MAN, AND APPARENTLY QUITE A FAN OF MINE."
"HE TOLD ME EVERYTHING!"
"HE WAS VERY GLAD TO HEAR YOU WERE IN GOOD HANDS AS MY ASSISTANT!"
I AM NOT YOUR ASSISTANT.
YOU TRIED TO KILL ME.
SEE? THAT'S WHY PARTNERS SHOULDN'T KEEP SECRETS FROM ONE ANOTHER!
I DON'T. NOT FROM MY REAL PARTNERS.
OH? SO THESE PLAYERS KNOW WHO YOU ARE?
NO. NO THEY DON'T.

EANWHILE—
SIR!
SOMETHING ON THE NIGHT SCOPE?
YESSIR— SOMETHING MOVING UP THE EAST ROAD.
SOME THING?
DON'T KNOW WHAT IT IS, BUT IT'S BIG AND FAST!
SHOULD BE COMIN' UP NEAR THE FIVE LENGTHS MARK.
NEVER A GOOD COMBINATION.
WELL, LET'S— WHOA!
THAT'S DAMN FAST!
RING THE BELL—
—AND GET SOME ARCHERS TO THE EAST GATE.
RED FIRE! ARE YOU SPARKSONS DEAF?
CLOSE THE DAMN GATE!
BUT...BUT ASSIA VELICHOU AND PAVEL DAKAR ARE STILL OUTSIDE!
THEY'RE HUNTING MUSHROOMS!
HUNTING—?! YOU CRETINS!
THEY GOT THREE MINUTES TO GET DRESSED—
—AND BACK INSIDE BEFORE YOU CLOSE THE GATE!
WHAT? BUT WE CAN'T—
THREE MINUTES!
WHAT'S COMING?
I DON'T KNOW, BUT YOU'D BETTER HOPE IT KILLS YOU—
—OR ELSE ASSIA'S FATHER WILL—
S-SIR—
I VISH TO ENTER THIS TOWN.

THE... THE TOWN IS... *CLOSED*...UNTIL *DAWN.*
BUT THE GATE IZ *NOT* CLOSED.
I MERELY SEEK—
TUNG!
THUP!
I FORGIVE.
ONCE.
SNAP!
NOW—
FIRE!
NO!

CK AT THE SHOW—
LOOK. I'M ONLY GOING TO EXPLAIN THIS ONCE.
THE WULFENBACHS THINK I'M DEAD.
REALLY.
THATS... GOOD.
I CAN'T SURVIVE AS A HETERODYNE.
I CAN'T EVEN SURVIVE AS A SPARK.
SO I WON'T. I'M DONE WITH ALL OF THAT. FINISHED.
AND I AM NOT GOING TO GO OFF HERO-ING WITH YOU. UNDERSTAND?
RHAAARRR!
IEE!
WHAT ON EARTH IS THAT?
RUN!
CRASH!
AH!

SLICE
I ONLY VISH TO—
CRUNCH!
RHAAA
!
AAH!
BLAZFT!

WHAT? BUT—WHERE DID IT—
SMASH!
NO!
AAAAH!
SMAK!
CRUNCH!
UND NOW VE SEE VOT HAPPEN TO CLEVER LITTLE HAND—
—VOT PLAY VITH NASTY TOYS

HA! THAT'S MY ASSISTANT, THANK YOU!
BOOT!
AK!
YOU-
AGATHA! RUN!
RHAA
PROBLEMS?

SOMEONE'S ATTACKING THE TOWN.
I'LL CUT YOU DOWN.
YOU'LL GET HER OUT OF HERE BEFORE YOU ESCAPE.
YES.
AND YOU'LL LEAVE THE TOWNSPEOPLE ALONE.
YES...
SWEAR.
SWEAR ON YOUR LOYALTY TO THE HOUSE OF HETERODYNE.
HEH.
GOOD VUN.
SHMOT GURL.
VE SO SVEAR— MISTRESS.
I'D BETTER BE RIGHT ABOUT YOU.
TOO LATE TO VORRY ABOUT DOT NOW, SVEETHOT!
AND NOW, HYU ANNOYING—
SCHTOP!
HYU HORR'BLE MONSTER-Y TING OF EVIL!
...VOT?

ER...
VE IZ JÄGERKIN CHARGED BY THE ANCIENT CONTRACT—
—VIT' DE JOB OV SAVIN' ALL DESE PEOPLE!
YAH! BY GETTIN' HYU OUT O' HERE!
NOW—IZ HYU GONNA RUN OR IZ HYU GONNA DIE?
TOSS!
HA!
DIS VILL SLOW HYU DOWN!
THUD.
SORRY— VOS VE SUPPOSED TO CATCH HIM?
I DUNNO / DON'T LIKE HIM
VATEVER! VE GOTS A MONSTER HUNT!
VE HUNT!

TER—
YOU SEE— MEONE CUT HEM DOWN.
ONE OF THOSE SHOW PEOPLE!
SIR! WE FOUND WHERE THE BEAR WENT!
IT SMASHED CLEAN THROUGH THE SOUTH GATE!
YOU CAUGHT THEM BY PLAYING HANGMAN?
JÄGERS LOVE TO PLAY GAMES—
—BUT THEY'RE FUZZY ON THE RULES.
HEY! THE SERGEANT SAYS WE CAN FIX OUR WAGON IN TOWN FOR FREE!
REALLY?!
GREAT! AND I'VE GOT A FRAU VELICHOU HERE WHO WANTS US TO PERFORM AT A WEDDING!
A GOOD THING, EH, MAYOR?
BUT NOW O-ONE WILL IN THE BET!
...ALSO A GOOD THING, I THINK.
BAH! I TRUST YOU KNOW WHAT TO DO THEN?
ALREADY DONE.
SOMETHING YOU SHOULD REMEMBER AS YOU FIGHT EVIL.
I TOLD YOU. I'M NOT DOING THAT.
YOU CAN'T MAKE ME.
MAKE YOU?
HA! HA! HA! HA!
WHAT?
YOU RAN STRAIGHT AT THE DANGER WITHOUT EVEN THINKING.
THAT'S WHO AND WHAT YOU ARE.
YOU SAY YOU WANT A NORMAL LIFE.
WE ALL SAY THAT AT ONE TIME OR ANOTHER.
YOU DESERVE YOUR CHANCE AT IT.
I'LL BE BACK N ABOUT THREE MONTHS—
—AND WE'LL SEE HOW "NORMAL" YOU ARE.
SMEK!
BUT SINCERELY— GOOD LUCK.
THE BUSTED CLANK
HOW CAN SOMEONE SO STUPID BE SO SMART?
HE ONLY SEES WHAT HE WANTS TO SEE.
WHICH IS WHY HE'S COMPLETELY WRONG ABOUT ME.
AH. RIGHT.
OF COURSE.

AH. FÜST. WHO IZ A GOOD BEAR?
WHUMF
HOKAY— I KNOW YOU EEDIOTS IZ THERE.
COME ON OUT.
IZ YOU SERIOUSLY TELLING ME—
DOT VE FOUND A HETERODYNE?
HO, YES.
IT'Z A GURL.
THE SMELL
THE VOICE-
SHE IZ O THE BLOODLI
DERE IS NO MISTAKE
A GURL?
DOT IZ... SURPRISIN
HYU THREE VILL STAY VITH HER.
IZ DOT ALL?
OUR TASK VAS TO FIND A HETERODYNE.
THIS WE HAF DONE.
NOW DE QVESTION IS—VOT IS TO BE DONE VIT HER?
YOU GOTS TO ASK?!
IT HAZ BEEN TOO LONG.
I VANT INSTRUCTIONS.
UNTIL DEN, KEEP HER ALIVE.

'O BE CONTINUED IN: GIRL GENIUS® Book FIVE:

AGATHA HETERODYNE & THE CLOCKWORK PRINCESS

READ NEW COMICS THREE TIMES A WEEK AT:

WWW.GIRLGENIUS.NET

WANT TO HEAR A STORY?
YEAH! A HETERODYNE BOYS STORY!
BUT TELL IT *RIGHT*, MARY!
DON'T MESS IT UP THIS TIME.
OKAY, HOW ABOUT...
"*THE TURBINES OF ATLANTIS?*"
Fan Fiction
Story: Shaenon K. Garrity
Pictures: Phil Foglio
Colors: Cheyenne Wright
"I KNOW *TURBINES OF ATLANTIS!*"
"THAT'S A GOOD ONE!"
BILL & BARRY HETERODYNE
LAD YOU PPROVE.
O THE HETERODYNE YS WERE CROSSING THE ATLANTIC,
N THEIR WAY TO SHUT DOWN THE MAD RFUMERIES OF HAITI..."
THE *WAVE-WALKER* WORKS EVEN BETTER THAN WE PLANNED!
WE'LL BE PUTTING THAT ARMY OF *SCENT ZOMBIES* TO REST BY SUPPER!
BILL! *LOOK!*

A SEA MONSTER!
NO, A CLANK—
THE BIGGEST I'VE EVER SEEN!
GRAAAA
WE'D BETTER LOOK INTO THIS, BARRY.
PASS ME THE HARPOON CANNON!
WE JETTISONED IT TO LIGHTEN THE CRAFT!
REMEMBER?
NO NEED TO FEAR!
MARIA ANTONIA FANTASIA PHILOMEL
WILL DISMANTLE THIS BRUTE!
"MARY!

AH! ARIETTA!
YOU'RE AS BOLD AND BEAUTIFUL AS YOU WERE THE DAY WE RESCUED YOU FROM THE BANDITS WHO KIDNAPPED YOU—
AFTER YOUR MYSTERIOUS YET FAMOUSLY POWERFUL SPARK TRIBE WAS COMPLETELY WIPED OUT,
LEAVING YOU THE ONLY HEIR TO ITS SECRETS!
OH, ENOUGH ABOUT MY TRAUMATIC PAST!
I WAS ALSO A PRINCESS!
ALL THAT MATTERS NOW IS THAT I RESCUE YOU—
WITH THIS ICE RAY I HAPPEN TO HAVE JUST INVENTED!
"MARY!"
WHAT?
YOU ALWAYS PUT YOUR OWN STUPID CHARACTERS IN THE STORY
AND MESS IT ALL UP!
YOU'RE DOING IT AGAIN!
THAT'S NOT THE WAY IT GOES!
I'M JUST TRYING TO SPICE THINGS UP.
WELL, DON'T!
OKAY, OKAY.
ALL WE'VE GOT ARE THE NET GUNS AND GAS MASKS—
WE BROUGHT TO USE AGAINST THE SCENT ZOMBIES!
CAN WE REPURPOSE THEM IN TIME?
WE'VE GOT TO TRY!
AIR
AIR

AND FAST! HERE SHE BLOWS!
WHOOM
CHOMP CHOMP
QUICK! THE BOLT CUTTERS!
NO NEED!
TA-DA!
MARIETTA NO!
WITH A FEW MINOR ADJUSTMENTS, THE GAS MASK CAN BE USED FOR UNDERWATER—
DANGER
"MARY, THIS HA BETTER NOT BE
WHP!
IT'S TOO DANGEROUS!
KA-CHUNK!
KABOOM!

MARIETTA!
SHE—SHE MADE THE ULTIMATE SACRIFICE FOR US...
WE DIDN'T *DESERVE* HER!
WORST OF ALL,
I NEVER GOT TO TELL HER MY *TRUE FEELINGS!*
NO, BILL...
YOUR LOVE AND THE MYSTIC AMULET I ALWAYS CARRY HAVE *REVIVED* ME...
MARIETTA!
I NEVER THOUGHT I'D SEE YOUR STUNNING VIOLET EYES AGAIN!
WAIT— THEY'RE *SILVER* NOW...
THEY CHANGE COLOR.
OH, MARIETTA...
"MOOOOM!!"

MARY'S *RUINING* THE HETERODYNE BOYS!
IT DOESN'T *GO* LIKE THAT!
WHATEVER!
I'M GOING TO BED!
KIDS, KIDS.
YOUR SISTER *LOVES* TELLING YOU THOSE STORIES.
AND WHEN YOU GET DOWN TO IT,
WHAT'S MORE IMPORTANT—
WHAT THE HETERODYNE BOYS ACTUALLY *DID*...
OR THE *DREAMS* THEY INSPIRE IN US?
WHAT THEY *DID*.
DUH.
RIGHT.
BEDTIM
I *KNOW* HOW IT GOES.
THEY DIVE TO NEW ATLANTIS AND REVERSE THE SEVEN CORKSCREW TOWERS—
TO STOP THE SPARK EMPEROR OF THE DEEPEST TRENCH.
I JUST THOUGHT MY WAY WAS MORE *INTERESTING*.
True History of the Heterodynes
HETERODYNE TALES FOR THE HEARTHSIDE
THE HETERODYNE BOYS

CREEEK
MOM?
I'M SORRY...
I USED TO HAVE THEM BOTH FALL FOR A GIRL NAMED RAVEN MOONSDAUGHTER.
"Ardentia Verba"
KLIK
"Ardentia Verba"
END!

READ MORE COMICS ONLINE AT:
WWW.GIRLGENIUS.NET
MONDAY · WEDNESDAY · FRIDAY